Testimonials

"This is the most fun I have had reading a book in years. A fascinating roadmap for how technology will ignite a flame of creativity for all artists and fans." - *Roxanne Somboonsiri, Global Partnerships Lead, Facebook*

"Anthony McGuire is a visionary who speaks powerfully and lyrically about technology and culture - and the power of decentralization - in a way that few others can. I recommend this without hesitation." - *Hamdan Azhar, Lead Data Scientist at Zap and Global Blockchain Evangelist*

"Stop whatever you are doing and read this book. Anthony has inspired me to care about blockchain technology and I know it's just the beginning." - *Devika Wood, Founder of Vida Care, Forbes 30 Under 30*

"I strongly recommend anyone who may be interested in the music ecosystem and what blockchain may disrupt to read Anthony's book. I just hope more people like Anthony would direct their energy and wisdom to disrupt the music industry on the basis of putting artists in the centre." - *Leslie Ching, Music Industry Veteran, former CEO of OneStop Asia (joint venture of 3 major record labels Universal, Warner, and Sony)*

"This is a fascinating book on blockchain and music. So exciting to see this type of analysis!" - *Vanessa Bakewell, Entertainment Vertical Lead, Facebook*

"Translating technical subjects into messages people can understand is a difficult task. Anthony accomplishes this and manages to create thoughtful dialogue on the future of music, entertainment, and technology." - *Deven Patel, PhD, Ads Research, Snap Inc.*

"This book helps you understand how blockchain technology can create an exciting new future for sports and entertainment. It's an essential read about how you should think differently about engaging your fanbase." - *Koen Bosma, Director of Qatar Sports Tech Accelerator, Former Professional Football Player*

"In a world where technology has an increasing impact on the fabric of society, we need voices like Anthony to help us make sense of technological comlpexity. Every industry should be aware of the potential of tech to completely transform the way things are done." - *Alvin Carpio, CEO of The Fourth Group, Forbes 30 Under 30*

"Anthony gives a very good introduction to blockchain/DLT use in the music industry. I learnt a lot about the music industry that I didn't know before and there is clear potential for DLT to impact in the sector." - *Nikhil Vadgama, Deputy Director (Acting), University College London Centre for Blockchain Technologies*

"In his book, Anthony entertains, educates, and inspires you. I read the book in one go and felt motivated to think more deeply about innovation within the music industry throughout the entire reading." - *Daniel Dippold, President of Kairos Society Europe*

"This book delves into the enigmatic subject of blockchain in an extraordinarily clear and enjoyable way." - *Greg West, Head of Programmatic Advertising, Global & DAX*

"Anthony's delightful book is a genuine blend of the arts and technology, oozing with eye-opening insight and relevant inspiration for all types of creatives. Bravo." - *Ken Uehara, Award Winning Director, UNiDAYS, UNILAD*

"Amid increasing scrutiny and skepticism about utility tokens on the back of infamous fraud cases across the globe, Anthony McGuire puts a strong case forward in favour of tokenising music rights, reminding us of the enabling power of blockchain and smart contracts to change inefficient industries overcrowded by intermediaries." - *Guilherme Silva, Research Associate, Centre for Technology and Global Affairs at University of Oxford*

To my Mom and Dad.

Music On The Chain:

A Story of Blockchain, The New Frontier of Creativity

By

Anthony McGuire

Table of Contents

Anthony McGuire is a passionate fan of blockchain technology and co-founder of Frontier X, a technology venture studio. Anthony previously worked on Facebook's Global Partnerships team in both New York and London, managing some of the world's largest Fortune 500 clients including American Express, Procter & Gamble, Renault-Nissan, and Heineken. Prior to Facebook, Anthony worked at Singularity University in Silicon Valley. He was first alto saxophone in middle school, lead guitarist for a death metal band, singer in an award-winning international choir, and is now a Soho House DJ. He is deeply interested in the intersection of arts and technology and has spoken about the topic in places ranging from The University of Oxford, Ohio Wesleyan University in Delaware, Ohio, The National University of Science and Technology in Islamabad, Pakistan, and Victoria University in Wellington, New Zealand. Anthony is originally from New Zealand but has lived, studied, and worked in Japan, Russia, the Philippines, India, Indonesia, the United States, and the UK. Anthony currently lives in London and spends most of his time immersed in books, music, or films.

1. The Wu Tang Clan & Martin Shkreli

"No matter how corrupt, greedy, and heartless our government, our corporations, our media, and our religious and charitable institutions may become, the music will still be wonderful."

-Kurt Vonnegut

A Music Industry Microcosm

In December 2015, notorious pharmaceutical executive and former hedge fund manager Martin Shkreli bought the only existing copy of the latest Wu-Tang Clan album off the online auction site Paddle8. The Wu-Tang Clan, one of the world's leading hip hop groups, had released the album *Once Upon a Time in Shaolin* as part performance-art/part-political statement. In a world where most people don't even pay for music, Robert "RZA" Diggs, defacto leader of the Wu-Tang Clan, wanted to challenge the public's perception of how music should be valued. With only one album copy in existence, RZA intended to make a public critique about how fans approach music today. He saw a world where people frivolously download song after song without considering the welfare of the original artist. As an artistic experiment meant to confront the current state of music, RZA made only one copy of the latest Wu-Tang album and released it through a private, online auction.

It's arguable whether RZA has accomplished his goal of making the right statement to improve the music industry. Martin Shkreli paid $2 million for the album, including all accompanying legal rights to the album's distribution. This was the most expensive record ever sold and made Shkreli the sole owner with complete control over the album's release. Some of the people featured on the album include the singer Cher, Game of Thrones actress Carice Van Houten, and a few players from FC Barcelona. Technically, 50% of the album is still owned by RZA and Tarik "Civalringz" Azzougarh, the lead Wu-Tang Clan producer who first conceptualised the idea behind *Once Upon a Time in Shaolin*. The contract stipulates that the buyer (Shkreli) cannot resell the album until 88 years after the purchase, which will be the year 2103. The number 88 was chosen to symbolise the 8 original members of the Wu-Tang Clan, the concept of infinity and also represent the Wu-Tang Clan's broader interest in *"numerology, mathematics, and symbolism to the things we do."* At one point, there was even a rumour spreading around the internet that a clause within the contract stated that the Wu-Tang Clan and actor Bill Murray would be the only people allowed to 'steal back' the album, with no legal repercussions. After the album was sold, Warren Patterson, the photographer who shot the album's cover art, filed a lawsuit against the Wu-Tang Clan, claiming the photo was used without his permission and that he did not receive any payment for his work. This undoubtedly remarkable story elicited a mixture of both positive and negative reactions from Wu-Tang fans.

Martin Shkreli came into mainstream consciousness through his controversial decision to raise the price of Daraprim, a drug used to treat rare conditions related to HIV/AIDS and cancer patients. His company Turing Pharmaceuticals had acquired the license to the drug in 2015 and raised the price from $13.50 per pill to $750 per pill. Shkreli became the public face of the company and defended the decision by explaining how the additional profits would be used to fund further research & development efforts. Martin's controversial behaviour and prolific use of social media resulted in news outlets giving him the name "Pharma Bro" and calling him the "most-hated man in America." In one particularly notable incident, Martin Shkreli offered a $5,000 reward for anyone who could get a strand of Hilary Clinton's hair after she had publicly criticised him over Twitter.

Shkreli also has a long history with the hip hop industry. Through a series of tweets, he once offered to buy exclusive ownership rights to Kanye West's 2016 album *The Life of Pablo* for $10 million. On another occasion, he offered to bail rapper Bobby Shmurda out of jail. Right after purchasing *Once Upon a Time in Shaolin*, Shkreli also got involved in a public feud with Wu-Tang Clan member Ghostface Killah. At certain points over the past few years, Shkreli teased the internet by claiming he would release the Wu-Tang Clan album in exchange for sexual favours from Taylor Swift or if Donald Trump became President of the United States. After Donald Trump's election, Martin Shkreli played a few seconds of the album on a YouTube livestream but the full album still has not been released to the public. In an interview with Bloomberg, RZA said about Shkreli, "*He bought it, he can do what he wants. Art--the beautiful thing about art, from my standpoint, is that it has no discrimination. What we've done is historical, and you can't remove that.*"

Shkreli was convicted of securities fraud in 2017 and U.S. District Judge

Kiyo Matsumoto ordered the court to seize $7.3 million worth of Shkreli's assets, including a Picasso painting, his shares in Vyera Pharmaceuticals, an enigma machine from World War Two, and $5 million in cash from his E-Trade brokerage account. Oddly enough, another asset in Shkreli's possession was then unreleased hip hop album *Tha Carter V* from rapper Lil Wayne. The album was meant to be released in 2014, but was then postponed for several years due to legal disputes between Lil Wayne and his record label Cash Money Records. *Tha Carter V* has since been released on September 28, 2018.

What is going to happen to the Wu-Tang album and the rest of the assets seized from Shkreli? The official statement from the United States District Court for the Eastern District of New York was "*The United States hereby gives notice of its intent to dispose of the forfeited property in such manner as the United States Attorney General may direct.*" It's unclear what exactly this means for the album's release, and yet implies that it may require United States Attorney General to have the final say on what happens. The fate of *Once Upon a Time in Shaolin* hangs in the balance. While at one point Martin Shkreli was the world's sole gatekeeper of the latest Wu-Tang Clan album, it now lies in the hands of the government.

There are many ways to describe this saga - bizarre, outrageous, frustrating. Regardless of your personal opinion, it is most instructive to use this Wu-Tang Clan—Martin Shkreli situation as a broader metaphor for the messiness within the music industry. Artists are struggling to figure out a way to release and profit from their music. Some fans suffer and others fans benefit as a result of this. And the role of record labels in this equation is constantly being questioned. Challenges exist for artists, fans, and record labels.

2. Introducing Blockchain

"The future belongs to those who believe in the beauty of their dreams."

-Eleanor Roosevelt

Why You Should Care

As a fan of the Wu-Tang Clan, I really want to hear their new album. I also understand that the problems associated with the album's release are problems associated with the entire music industry. The music industry should be able to evolve with the latest developments in technology to solve these problems. Technology can provide modern solutions to modern challenges and blockchain is a modern solution that can help both fans and artists in three ways: Traceability, Compensation, and Tokenisation. Things that previously were not possible are now on the road to mass adoption.

How does blockchain work for the music industry?

- **Blockchain + Traceability** = An improved way to trace digital music and intellectual property around the internet.

- **Blockchain + Compensation** = More effective, easier, and efficient ways to compensate people for their music.

- **Blockchain + Tokenisation** = New methods to fund artwork and build direct artist-to-fan relationships.

First we need to ask - what is a 'Blockchain'? At the time of this writing (October 2018), many people are aware of blockchain as a buzzword but do not have a deep, practical understanding of the technology. To some, blockchain is the grandest socio-political-economic revolution of the 21st Century. To others, blockchain and cryptocurrencies are the greatest scam of the digital era. A measured approach to understanding this technology requires you to accept that the reality lies somewhere in the middle.

There are three main terms you need to understand here:

1) **Blockchain**

2) **Smart Contracts**

3) **Tokenisation**

Blockchain

Take a step back and imagine yourself in ancient Egypt five thousand years ago. You are the wealthy ruler of the people, the pharaoh, and all of your wealth is in gold bars, 1 million gold bars. You are traveling across the desert and have 1000 camels each carrying 1000 gold bars (1,000 x 1,000 = 1,000,000). This basically works, but it is a very inconvenient, unwieldy process to manage these thousand camels and so you ask yourself if there is a better way. Imagine that instead of you having 1000 camels carrying 1000 gold bars each, you could convert those gold bars into cash.

These cash notes are lighter and easier to transport—so now you only need

100 camels and each of those camels carries the cash equivalent of 10,000 gold bars (100 x 10,000 = 1,000,000). Managing 100 camels is a lot less stressful for you, which makes you happier and thankful for the invention of cash. Over time, you continue to seek improvements in the efficiency of how you manage your wealth and one day technology progresses to the point where you have the internet. Now you can convert that cash into digital cash you store on one computer. You now only need one camel to carry the one computer that stores all of your digital money. This is a rough analogy for the evolution of money across history.

That is the state of the world today. All of your different types of data are conveniently stored by one entity, or one 'camel.' Your financial data, how much money you have, is stored in the database of your bank. Your identity data, documents proving who you are, is stored in the database of your government. Your online behavioural data, records of what you are browsing and purchasing online, is stored in the databases of the largest consumer internet companies like Facebook, Amazon and Google.

So let's take this version of you as modern day Egyptian pharaoh and think about how you would carry around your wealth today. You have one camel carrying one computer across the desert that keeps a digital record of your financial wealth. Now imagine that you take that digital data, make a thousand digital copies and store them on a thousand different camels around the world. One thousand different camels around the world are each storing a copy of your financial data. Those thousand camels represent the fact that you now have a decentralised, distributed world supercomputer holding your data. You now have what is essentially a blockchain. Each camel holding a copy of your data around the world is a different 'block' and they are 'chained' together across the internet to maintain your data.

Let us think about the decentralised, distributed characteristics of a blockchain in a different way. Here is an analogy you will appreciate: storing data on a blockchain is similar to the way Voldemort's horcruxes worked in the Harry Potter novels. In the famous fiction series, the evil villain Voldemort has fragments of his soul stored within seven different artifacts around the world, which are called horcruxes. Instead of keeping his soul in one place, he kept it in seven places to make it more difficult for his enemies to attack him. You would

have to destroy all seven horxcruxes to kill Voldemort. Destroying just one

horcrux would still keep the overall 'network' of his soul alive. These horcruxes

are functioning like a a blockchain. You could say that the horcruxes, with their

powers combined, were a *decentralised, distributed* database. And the data

within that database was the content of Voldemort's soul. If you think about

storing copies of your financial data on several different databases instead of just

one database, there is more security in storing that data on a decentralised,

distributed blockchain database because there is no single point of failure.

The way you view data within the thousand camels, or the seven Voldemort

horcruxes, or the Bitcoin blockchain is like a shared spreadsheet. Whenever

someone makes a change to the shared spreadsheet or document, you can see all

the edits. That way you are all held accountable for any changes you make

because you can't make a change to any previous version of data without the

permission of everyone else. Blockchains hold these properties. You cannot

manipulate the data on a blockchain by yourself because the data is validated by

everyone participating in that blockchain. Nothing gets changed within the data without each participant reaching consensus, the process by which we all have to agree in order to edit data or process a transaction.

A blockchain is a type of decentralised, distributed database that stores information and is secured by cryptography. This type of database functions like a shared spreadsheet where all the data is available for people to see and the collective 'truth' of that data is verified by all the participants on that spreadsheet. Because each participant relies on every other participant to validate the data, you no longer need a third party to manage your data. Like a shared Google spreadsheet, the fact that we are all monitoring the same data means we better trust each other to enter data rather than relying on a third party to enter data on our behalf. It's a new way to store information. And while the concept of verifying and streamlining data doesn't scream out as a sexy problem, this can lead to a surprisingly large number of incredible opportunities.

For example, when you are sending money from your bank account to a friend's bank account, you are relying on your respective banks and a variety of intermediaries to serve as validators of the data. These middlemen are the ones handling the transaction from beginning to end. If you are using a shared blockchain database to replace the role of a third-party bank or intermediary, you can send money directly from one person to another more quickly and efficiently, with a new degree of trust between you and the recipient. Because of this concept, people have been able to create cryptocurrencies like Bitcoin, a *"peer-to-peer version of electronic cash [that] allows online payments to be sent directly from one party to another without going through a financial institution."* The mysterious 'Satoshi Nakamoto' wrote the Bitcoin white paper in 2008 to explain this idea and his words have since served as the foundation of the blockchain industry.

People are actively experimenting with different ways that blockchain can be applied to solve problems:

Supply Chain

Supply chains are the sequence of processes by which a product moves from initial supplier to end customer, such as the entire journey of coffee beans being first harvested by a farmer in Ethiopia to then becoming the double espresso you order at a cafe in Los Angeles; or the complex process through which Apple sources raw materials to manufacture their iPhones in China and then distributes them to Apple stores around the world. These processes are complicated, messy, and often old-fashioned.

Putting all the data involved in a supply chain onto a blockchain would make the whole process more transparent. You could have greater accountability and be able to turn an analog paper trail into a digital blockchain data trail. For certain goods, this shared blockchain would help decrease counterfeiting, lower operational costs, and improve the legality of the process. With every transaction and step of a supply chain recorded on a blockchain, you are improving the process for all parties involved.

Supply chains need to be solid for orders and deliveries to be predictable. Corporations closely manage their supply chains to make sure food items are kept safe and uncontaminated. Storing that supply chain data on a blockchain would enable all the involved stakeholders to have a clearer, traceable view of their products. If you are mining precious minerals, having the data secured on a blockchain can help you verify whether the mining process involved any grossly illegal activity like child labour. Many companies with large supply chains are currently testing blockchain technology - such as Walmart for their food supply, De Beers for diamond mining, and Maersk for shipping.

Digital Identity Ownership

If a single, secure, decentralised blockchain database could hold all of your information, you would not need to keep different copies of your identity with different agencies. Right now, a certain governmental organisation keeps a record of your passport, another public entity keeps a record of your driver's license, and your university will keep a record of your academic degree. The unsexy problem of separated databases actually incurs lot of cost, time, and effort, most notably in the associated paperwork and operations. If you could put your passport, your drivers license, and all other major forms of identification on a single blockchain, it would be much easier for you to manage and share. The data wouldn't necessarily be stored on the databases of these different agencies, but on your own blockchain database. In that sense, the data and metadata attached to your identity would actually be 'owned' by you for the very first time.

You could have a greater say in the way your data is used. You can have more control over the data that different internet companies currently use to monetise your attention or serve you advertising. You could more easily vote in local elections or apply for a mortgage since your digital identity is now more easily accessible and has been validated. You may no longer need to carry around physical copies of your driver's license or passport and you can eliminate the laborious process of getting new copies of these documents from government agencies like the Department of Motor Vehicles (DMV), your local embassy, or your university registrar office.

Smart Contracts

Smart contracts are digital contracts or legal agreements that are written into computer code and executed dynamically. This doesn't necessarily remove the need for lawyers or currently existing arbiters, but this can save money and add more efficiency to the currently manual process of traditional paper contracts. Smart contracts are *self-executing*, meaning that since the conditions of the contract are enforced through computer code, the contract's terms will be automatically executed whenever the programmed software decides legal conditions are met.

Efficiency

Contracts are legal agreements between two parties that create certain conditions. Right now, these parties operate in the real world and a large part of contract drafting, amendment, and editing is a manual process involving hours of physical work and paper resources. Purely from an operational efficiency perspective, making all of those contracts digital will save money not just for law firms but anyone dealing with contracts. Removing time and cost from paper processes at banks, law firms, and government agencies will save the entire world a lot of money. Transactions in general can happen with less of a need for facilitation between lawyers and courts. Subjectivity still plays a large role in settling legal disputes, but you can't sneakily make changes to a smart contract like you could to a physical contract because there is a traceable digital record of the smart contract hosted on a blockchain.

Compensation

If you can trust that verified terms of a contract are legitimate, you can have the automatic facilitation of financial payments through smart contracts. Eliminating the need of a central party to serve as a verifier would lead to more competition, better services, and cheaper prices. Imagine you are renting an apartment on Airbnb, you can have your money held in digital escrow until you actually unlock a box containing the key to the apartment. When the 'terms' of that contract are met, i.e. you gaining physical access to the apartment, the distribution of funds to the apartment owner would happen instantly. As the owner of that Airbnb, you don't need to manage this process from your end since all of these terms are placed into a digital smart contract. Putting aside Airbnb, just renting in general can happen more quickly without the need for a broker since their role as financial middlemen is diminished. Online wire transfers right now can take several days, but would happen in seconds through a smart contract and only if your desired legal conditions are met. This can change the levels of variability and uncertainty we have in accounting. Why have something like rent paid on a monthly, fixed basis? If facilitating payments between two parties can happen with nearly zero friction, maybe you can have more flexibility with payments on a peer-to-peer level. Imagine a smart contract that automatically pays you for your services as a plumber as soon as the job has been completed, as per the conditions of your client. Imagine a smart contract that automatically collects the rent from your property so you don't have to chase each of your tenants individually. The pain and occasional danger of paper invoicing can be diminished. All forms of payment and financial transaction become easier to manage.

Tokenisation

As a result of blockchain technology, you are now able to create digital assets and cryptocurrencies like Bitcoin. The technology has spurred on the creation of hundreds of other cryptocurrencies and platforms, all focusing on their own respective use case. Cryptocurrency tokens are generated and then released through a particular event often called a token sale, token generation event or initial coin offering (ICO). ICOs have been used to launch completely new cryptocurrencies but also to tokenise currently existing real-world assets, creating digital representations in the form of crypto tokens. There has been a large movement towards the idea of *tokenisation*, which essentially means creating a unique, digital representation of value of something in the real world. Bitcoin is a digital representation of monetary value. Much like shares in a publicly listed company are essentially 'created' as a representation of company value, crypto tokens are 'created' as a digital representation of company value. These advancements can result in a handful of small revolutions in financial democratisation.

Fundraising

The fundraising process for technology startups is immensely difficult. Most of the largest, most successful tech companies of the past few decades have relied on funding from venture capital (VC) firms. While VCs certainly deserve credit for enabling the creation of large tech companies, many structural issues exist within the VC industry. Women receive only 2% of venture funding and minorities get an even smaller percentage. There are inherent biases towards young, white males from elite universities like Stanford or MIT as their backgrounds are similar to the VCs funding them. Many Silicon Valley VCs have refused to invest in companies outside of the San Francisco Bay Area, adding another layer of cultural and geographic bias to fundraising. Even Vinod Khosla, one of the world's most famous VCs has said that 80-90% of VCs add negative value. Fundraising itself is a full-time job that takes away time from you building your core business as an entrepreneur. In return for VC funding, you often have to sign away large stakes of equity in your company. The VC has all the leverage since there are not many other funding options to grow your business, until now.

This is one of the reasons why crowdfunding has become more popular and why platforms like AngelList have been able to further democratise the fundraising process. Crowdfunding is the process by which you open up your fundraising round to people online, the crowd. Websites like Kickstarter, Indiegogo, or Seedrs have enabled people to fund their own businesses or creative projects by soliciting relatively small contributions from a relatively large group of people rather than a centralised entity like a VC firm. AngelList

offers a similar service, functioning as a marketplace for startups to raise

investment from angel investors—affluent investors that can provide more

capital than most people but still not at the size of a venture capital firm.

Considering that most VC firms prioritise investing in high tech companies, the

platform of crowdfunding and the market of angel investors can also diversify

into funding more traditional small businesses, ones that have been considered

'less exciting' than your typical Silicon Valley startup.

ICOs are taking the democratisation of fundraising one step further. Pretty

much anyone can create an ICO to raise funds for their company through selling

crypto tokens. The free market can decide whether projects should be funded and

at what levels. By creating a public ICO, you could literally be receiving

investment from farmers in rural Indonesia, or professors in Chile, or rappers in

Slovakia. This level of access to capital in order to create your business is truly

groundbreaking. When used appropriately and subject to regulation, tokenising

your company and raising funds could empower all types of global businesses.

Fractional Ownership

Tokenisation allows you to create a digital representation of any asset and divide it into very small denominations. For example, we can look at tokenisation applied to real estate. Real estate is an extremely important investment opportunity. Let's say you have a $100 million apartment building consisting of ten apartments, with each individual apartment priced at $10 million. For most people, paying $10 million for an apartment is far too expensive, and so the asset class of luxury real estate is not within their grasp. High value real estate, as has been the case traditionally, remains within the reach of only the wealthiest people in society. If you took that $100 million apartment building and 'tokenised' it, you would then be creating a digital representation of that same property by creating 100 million tokens at $1 each. Someone can benefit from the fractional ownership of an expensive apartment building by paying only $100 for 100 tokens of the broader real estate asset. If the value of the apartment building increases over time, your 100 tokens should also increase in value—a much more accessible investment for more people than purchasing a $100 million apartment building. You can apply this same principle of tokenisation to fine art, music, or almost any physical good. Maybe you own an apartment, but need more liquidity, and don't necessarily want to sell your entire apartment for money. You could sell fractional ownership of your apartment in exchange for tokens. You could tokenise yourself as an artist and sell tokens that represent a percentage of your royalties. I could tokenise my book collection and sell tokens to my friends, giving them partial ownership. In theory, you could tokenise everything.

New Features, New Incentives

Now that we are able to attach different 'tokens' as a new representation of value for certain goods, this opens new possibilities. The way a crypto token *should* function has not yet been decided by society. This technology is brand new. The rules are yet to be written. A sportswear brand could create tokens that represent not only partial ownership of their company, but maybe exclusive features for token owners that incentivise them to be brand ambassadors. As a restaurant, you could have special menu items available only to people who have bought your tokens. As a charity, you could reward people in tokens for doing good deeds or participating in certain community service events. As a media outlet, you could allow anyone to access certain articles but have special sections of your publication where only token holders can read the content. You can create unique features attached to token ownership and subsequently create a brand new set of economic and personal incentives. Because tokens have a given price dependent on supply and demand, it is in your interest to see the price of that token increase and the attached restaurant, charity, or news outlet grow.

An infamous Newsweek article from 1995 called "Why The Web Won't Be Nirvana," was written by the scientist Clifford Stoll, who proceeded to outline why the hype around the internet will not result in any great transformational change. One of the key lines from his article says, "*Yet Nicholas Negroponte, director of the MIT Media Lab, predicts that we'll soon buy books and newspapers straight over the Internet. Uh, sure.*" Stoll was also the author of *Silicon Snake Oil: Second Thoughts on the Information Superhighway*, a book he published in 1996 that makes, among other claims, a strong argument against e-mail:

"Why not send a fax? It's far more universal than e-mail—we not only find fax machines everywhere, but they can all speak to one another...I find it easier

to just scribble a note on a plain piece of paper and send it over a fax. Or

address an envelope, lick a stamp, and mail a letter."

Practically speaking, fax machines and sending letters serve the same purpose as e-mail. They all accomplish the process of delivering a message from Person A to Person B. When your grandparents first saw e-mail, they probably didn't understand the hype because the exact same process of communication could be accomplished through other means. What they missed was that e-mail provided meaningful communication improvements in terms of efficiency and accessibility. E-mail was a much quicker way to send a message to someone than a fax, and the decreasing costs of computing and increasing portability of smartphones made this process significantly improve over time. This also resulted in second-order consequences such as easier ways to conduct cross-border business, outsource international customer service, or maintain long-distance romantic relationships. Efficiency and accessibility matter—it is the way that technology has nurtured the growth of civilisation over history.

You can decide to not do an ICO and instead create a crowdfunding campaign. However, an ICO can happen more quickly through the almost immediate cross-border transfer of cryptocurrencies and can allow investors from all around the world to participate. You can decide to not tokenise your real estate assets and instead refinance your mortgage. However, tokenisation creates new investment opportunities for people who previously could not afford real estate while still giving you rapid access to liquidity. You can decide to keep paying out your bills through traditional means and forget about smart contracts. However, a smart contract could take away stress and time from the process, and could dynamically adjust your payments higher or lower based on the services you are provided. The main point here is that blockchain technology can make a lot of currently existing processes much more efficient and accessible.

With this foundational knowledge about blockchain, let's move on to examine how the technology can be applied to the music industry for traceability, compensation, and tokenisation. There are a lot of cool things that previously could not be done before, but are now possible.

3. Music On A Blockchain

"There exist limitless opportunities in every industry. Where there is an

open mind, there will always be a frontier."

-Charles Kettering

Traceability

The problem of Traceability relates to data—how can data be recorded,

used, and monetised fairly? At the end of the day, music itself is raw data that is

disseminated online and then into our ears. Attached to that data is metadata

outlining the different people who created that music or are associated as

contributors. This data is important because it is a record of who owns the right

to that music and who should get paid for its usage. If we think of blockchain as

a sort of shared, universal spreadsheet to hold the world's data, it provides us

with a superior way to trace all important data ownership and attribution.

The music industry infrastructure around rights management is very messy and the process could improve to be more consistent, digital, and immutable. The music industry has tried coming together in the past to create a universal record in what was called the Global Repertoire Database. Unfortunately, this experiment failed and the project was shut down in 2014. Blockchain's utility as a universal, shared record of music data can be the novel solution to save the music industry.

When you release a song or album onto a public blockchain, think about the process as essentially releasing a music data file onto the internet for the whole world to see and access. Because the blockchain is an immutable public record, that means it is a validated public display of a master music data file and all associated information. If the RZA released *Once Upon a Time in Shaolin* onto the blockchain, that could serve as a global public record and he and his team would be credited as the true owners of the intellectual property. It's like we have all agreed to share a google doc with the same music information. This makes it harder for legal disputes to happen, since we are all able to look at the same data and you cannot make changes to the data on your own.

In this case, the ownership of the music is also decentralised, not controlled exclusively by record labels or streaming platforms but instead released onto a public blockchain not owned by one single person. At the other end of the spectrum, the most centralised form of 'music ownership' would be Martin Shkreli, who was able to hold an album hostage and prevent everyone else in the world from listening to it since he was the sole owner. While this is an extreme example, the way the music industry works now is between a fan like you and a musician like RZA, there exist several 'Martin Shkrelis' in the middle. Many middlemen exist between the artist and the fan, propping up the modern music industry.

Some of these Shkreli-like middlemen exist for RZA because they offer distribution and secure intellectual property. Record labels distribute RZA's music and organisations like the Recording Industry Association of America (RIAA) guarantee RZA's claims to music royalties. The internet has already made it easier for RZA to distribute music. Now the blockchain can help him protect his intellectual property. In a world where you have a public online record of all creative work available for everyone to see, your legal rights are publicly guaranteed. This open record keeping mechanism exists through a blockchain where we can trace the ownership of music back to the original artist.

Compensation

The problem of Compensation relates to how much an artist is actually being paid for their work. Artists can get paid by record labels, streaming services, royalty organisations and sometimes directly by fans. Each additional stakeholder an artist may have to deal with in order to get paid can make things more complicated. Complexity also exists when a musical composition has a large group of people who have worked together on a song in different capacities and with separate contractual agreements.

One of the challenges for musicians today is getting fair credit and compensation for their work. Currently, online streaming services are not very lucrative and illegal downloads are widespread. Royalty payments today are overseen by a variety of different organisations. Using smart contracts to encode currently existing legal structures on a blockchain would make it easier for these organisations to distribute royalties and allow artists to get paid more efficiently and frequently. As one of the producers of an album like *Once Upon a Time in Shaolin*, you may be entitled to a certain percentage of royalties. Transactions logged onto a public blockchain are underwritten by smart contracts, which are online legal agreements that can automatically execute contractual terms based on certain variables. So if smart contracts are programmed to include your legal rights to intellectual property, you can almost immediately receive royalties for every time the album is sold or played. Artists can automatically receive funds that are legally obligated to be distributed to them, more quickly. Not only would RZA receive the appropriate royalties for *Once Upon a Time in Shaolin*, but everyone else who worked on the album could receive royalties dynamically as people around the world enjoy the music. No more manual processes or filling out claim forms.

Collecting societies or performing rights organisations (PROs) are the organisations that collect royalties on behalf of musicians. To determine how much a musician should be paid, these collecting societies rely on a preposterous system of self-reporting. The collecting societies ask the owners of businesses like restaurants, shops, hotels or gyms to report what songs they play in a given week or month. This is contingent on the businesses having the mandatory license issued by the PRO to play music in the first place. Another option is for the businesses to apply for an annual music license fee to cover every song they play. The collecting society then makes a rough estimate of song plays based on sampling and the current popularity of different songs. This skews royalties in favour of the larger, better known artists. Considering how most people conduct their music listening informally, it's safe to assume that this system leaves enormous room for error and grossly undervalues the number of recorded plays per artist. Quite literally, legally and technically, you are breaking the law if you are playing music at work and using your personal Spotify account. The idea of royalty management is global, as most countries have their own collecting society with national-level responsibilities. As you might imagine with anything conducted internationally, there is inconsistency in terms of a country's data quality and varying practices between how each performing rights organisation operates on a national level. The process is extremely low tech, and while not everything needs to be at the frontier of technology, this outmoded methodology quite literally determines a large part of an artist's livelihood.

Another layer of messiness occurs when people seek licensing agreements, whether someone wants to allow their song to be used by someone else or whether you are seeking approval to use another song for your own project. The internet has brought distribution costs to zero—now anyone can take your song, put it up online, and the whole world could soon be listening to it without even paying you. While the laws of the music industry say that you need the appropriate licenses to play someone else's music, new platforms have made those rules easy to circumvent and many artists are missing out on compensation. Many major internet companies like Youtube are not held liable for copyright infringement due to the 1998 Digital Millennium Copyright Act (DMCA). Youtube cannot be held liable for copyright infringement since they essentially act as platforms for content that is uploaded by third parties. So long as the platforms have some kind of system to take down infringing content, like Youtube's three strikes rule, they can continue to host illegally uploaded music and claim 'Safe Harbour' against litigation. In 2018, almost 5 billion videos are watched on Youtube every day and 300 hours of content are uploaded every minute. If one of those videos is an illegal upload of your music, you need to go through a manual process of filling out a DMCA claim form that gets sent to Youtube. Considering the scale of content on Youtube, this DMCA claim solution is not scalable when applied to the internet and does not really help artists get paid fairly for their work.

The Music Modern Modernisation Act of 2018 was passed was signed into United States law on October 11, 2018. This piece of legislation attempted to address many of the modern challenges artists face in getting paid royalties. The law mandates that royalties include a song's producers when songs are played over satellite and online radio. The law includes provisions to streamline the music-licensing process to make it easier for rights holders to get paid when their music is streamed online. The law creates a single mechanical licensing database overseen by music publishers and songwriters, and establishes more rate standardisation. The Music Modernisation Act looked to improve how music licensing and royalties are paid to artists considering the advent of streaming services. Despite these efforts, legislation does not move at the speed of technology and cannot keep up with the complicated nature of the digital economy.

Even the most successful music technology companies of recent history, such as Spotify, have not solved these problems. Not only is Spotify regularly criticised for paying out artists very low levels of compensation per stream, but many major artists (e.g. Jay-Z, Beyonce, Garth Brooks) have completely boycotted Spotify and refused to put their music on the platform. The company is still a very impressive case study in technological innovation, but new approaches to compensating artists should always be examined. The more streamlined we can make these transactions, the more easily we can pay artists fairly and quickly. While streaming services continually conjure up controversy about providing an insufficient revenue stream for artists, there is at least more accuracy in measuring music played on streaming platforms. More advanced digital technology can better record how often music is played, which we can then store on a blockchain and then pay out royalties through smart contracts.

A recent article in Digital Music News cites some estimates that there are over $2.5 billion in unpaid music royalties due to inaccurate reporting. A specific

sub-category of technologies focuses on this specific problem, called Music

Recognition Technology or MRT. One of the most popular MRT products is

Shazam, a mobile app that can help you identify songs you hear in the

background. Artists are generally not equipped to solve this problem without the

help of technology to better record royalties. Advances in MRT hardware could

create digital IDs or 'fingerprints' of songs that could be placed onto a

blockchain and then correlate to royalty payments facilitated by smart contracts.

If you could have a digital ID attached to a song and then recorded onto a

blockchain, it's possible for you as an artist to account for almost every single

time your song is played commercially, or at the very least for the royalty

calculations to be significantly more accurate than the current system. And when

piracy and copyright infringement does occur, the process to make a DMCA

claim can, should, and likely will be automated. Or at the very least, technology

like artificial intelligence could be able to detect copyright infringement more

quickly and more accurately than manual DMCA takedown notices filed by

rights holders.

The artist Sixto Rodriguez is the subject of the 2012 documentary *Searching for Sugarman*. Rodriguez is a singer-songwriter from Detroit who released two albums in 1970 and 1971 under the label Sussex Records. Both albums, *Cold Fact* and *Coming From Reality*, sold poorly in the United States and Sussex Records ended up dropping Rodriguez soon afterwards. The record label closed down in 1975. After his short-lived music career in the early 1970s, Rodriguez worked in low-income physical labor jobs for the next three decades until the filming of the documentary revealed a remarkable story. The film explains how Rodriguez's music was bootlegged and found its way to South Africa, where Rodriguez eventually became as popular as Elvis. In a baffling example of real-life poetry, Rodriguez seemed to be completely unaware of the wild success his music had achieved outside of the United States. And most critically, this meant that Rodriguez received zero royalty payments for his music. Here is another heartwarming story that illustrates how music can transcend international borders, yet the business infrastructure supporting the precious talent of our favourite musicians like Rodriguez still deprived him of an income. The $2.5 billion estimate of unpaid music royalties sounds like a large number, but when you take one personal story like that of Rodriguez, you realise that there are likely tens of thousands of artists like him around the world who are missing out on wages and rewards for their creativity.

Tokenisation (and Relationships)

You can link the idea of tokenisation to a similar idea from history called patronage, where wealthy aristocrats or merchants paid artists to create works for them on a semi-permanent retainer or a set of subsidy-like financial grants. These wealthier individuals paying the artists were called 'patrons.' One of the most famous examples of patronage is the powerful Medici family of bankers and politicians. In 15th Century Italy, the family supported the arts by funding people such as the architect Brunelleschi to rebuild the Basilica of San Lorenzo in Florence in 1419. Their support extended to a variety of other artists like Michelangelo, Raphael, Donatello, and Leonardo Da Vinci.

The online platform Patreon was founded in 2013 and takes its name from the old idea of patronage. On Patreon, you can build relationships with artists and support them directly by paying them a fixed monthly amount. Catering primarily to videographers, artists, and writers, Patreon provides another revenue stream to people working in creative fields, a form of patronage for the digital age. Roughly 2 million 'patrons' have signed on to the platform to give some level of monthly contribution to the 100,000 content creators on Patreon, with the expected total of around $300 million in contributions over 2018. The idea behind Patreon makes a lot of sense, but could extend even further with blockchain tokenisation being used to provide more financial benefits to artists.

If you have a public record of music tied to the original artist and underpinned by smart contracts, you can streamline the modern process of patronage and maybe even create a new form of creative valuation. Tokenisation on the blockchain is the process of converting something from the real world into the digital world, represented by a cryptographic token you can purchase, use, or sell.

To use an example, imagine the Wu-Tang Clan creating Wu-Tang Tokens that you could buy as a fan. These aren't just shares in a company. These aren't just loyalty cards. These aren't just donations. A token combines all of them into one and places them on a blockchain. The artist and the fan have a variety of different benefits. As a fan, ownership of this token could grant you access to special Wu-Tang events or concerts, discounts on Wu-Tang merchandise, coupons for retail partnerships, membership in an exclusive Wu-Tang fan club, or a whole other realm of possibilities.

As an artist, you would have a stronger signal of people that are willing to support you financially as the price of the Wu-Tang Token in the open market is a function of supply and demand. It's not the same as owning a share of a company, but the token should be tied to the 'market value' of that artist and provide the token owner with useful services as well. The better the overall success of the Wu-Tang Clan, the higher the price of the token. If the group releases Wu-Tang sneakers, announces a world tour, or even releases a new album, the owners of the token would be more incentivised to support all of those activities. The Wu-Tang Token owners themselves will receive financial gains from broadly supporting their artists and serving as brand ambassadors. This also can serve as a feedback loop. If you keep track of the data coming from your token holder fans, you can glean more insight about the products and services you are putting out into the world. Your fans could voluntarily attach data to their token, like their demographics, interests, age, and other data points. These could serve to better personalise the goods and services you can sell them, providing a more tailored fan experience. This could be the future of all artist-fan relationships.

Having done a bit of research, I noticed that the son of Ol' Dirty Bastard from the Wu-Tang Clan is himself a hip hop artist called Young Dirty. A March 2018 article in Coindesk indicated that Young Dirty is launching a crypto token in honour of his father called Dirty Coin. This token will raise funds to support Young Dirty's musical projects, provide people access to certain concerts and enable them to buy merchandise. Another group of people have actually launched a Wu-Tang Coin to raise funds in order to buy back *Once Upon a Time in Shaolin* from Martin Shkreli, paying him in cryptocurrency. If the extended circle of Wu-Tang is already thinking about this, the time seems ripe for RZA to launch a Wu-Tang Token himself.

4. The Economics of Value

"I've learned that people will forget what you said, people will forget what you did, but people will never forget how you made them feel."

-Maya Angelou

People Value Things Differently

To better understand the grand implications of what blockchain could do for creative industries, it's worth taking a step back and thinking about economics. It's worth thinking about the choices we make in purchasing products and services. It's worth examining the idea of relative value.

In the economy, we are either buying things or selling things. Each buyer and seller has their own preferences about the price they are willing to pay or accept for a given product or service. Before any given transaction, the buyer has their own maximum price at which they are willing to buy a product and the seller has their own minimum price at which they are willing to sell a product. You may be willing to spend up to $50 on dinner tonight and not a dollar more. You may be willing to sell your old sofa for a minimum of $20 and will not accept anything lower. Our lives are full of these decisions on both sides of the transaction.

For example, if an artist (the seller) creates a painting and brings it to an art fair, she may put it on sale for $500 but be willing to negotiate down and sell it for as low as $300. If someone visiting the art fair sees that painting, she may want to pay $100 for the work but can go so far as to pay $300 for the painting. The point of sale is where both the buyer and seller end up after a negotiation, where they are willing to meet at a price that satisfies them both.

In almost every single situation, the point of desired purchase & desired sale for each person is not equal because people value things differently. So the price of a product is decided either through negotiation or the standard price is already set based on supply and demand.

For example, take the price of oranges:

- **Scenario 1**: You go to a supermarket that lists the price of oranges as $1.50 per orange. This is based on a variety of factors such as supermarket pricing policy, their current supply of oranges, and how much profit margin the store wants to make. You are not able to negotiate on price so you end up paying $1.50 for one orange. You are the buyer and the seller is the supermarket.

- **Scenario 2**: You go to a farmer's market where you are able to talk directly to the farmer who grows the oranges. While the farmer initially says that one orange costs $1.50, you are able to negotiate the price down to $1.00. You are the buyer and the farmer is the seller. OR, if you are a big fan of oranges and you are a big fan of the farmer, you may pay $2.00 because of your sheer enthusiasm for the product and the seller.

Conditions that affect your willingness to buy something are important - you might be starving for oranges after a long hiatus from orange eating, or you may have spent the last week overwhelmed at an orange festival and the last thing you want to see is another orange. In scenario 2, depending on how badly you are in the mood for oranges, you may have been willing to spend up to $5 for a bag of oranges. The farmer, for whatever reason, was willing to accept a price of $1.00. Price variation exists in scenario 2 because two people are able to deal with each other directly to appropriately price a transaction that works for both people.

Even though the buyers and sellers eventually agree on a price, in practice one person usually wins more value from the transaction relative to how much they truly value the product. We all value things differently. Whether based on our own personal preferences, past experience, or social environment, we are all unique and bring that uniqueness to making purchase decisions.

Why does this all matter? Because the study of economics and what economists do is aim to seek out the most optimal, efficient allocation of the world's resources. In a perfect free market economy, all prices would be dynamic and different based on factors like how much someone really wants a product.

If price was based more on relative supply and demand, we would have

more examples of surge pricing, a technique used by ride-sharing companies like

Uber. Surge pricing is a way of putting a price on a ride not based on a fixed rate,

but based on the dynamic movements of supply and demand within a given

economy. The two main groups of people who impact this are the *users* who

order the Ubers and the *drivers* who drive the cars. The drivers are *sellers* of a

service that is their driving and the passengers are the *buyers* of that service.

If there are hundreds of drivers available on the streets but just a dozen

passengers who want a ride, then the price of a ride would be low. There are

more drivers who offer jobs then there are passengers who *want* a ride = high

supply of drivers, low demand from passengers. And in the opposite scenario, if

there are hundreds of people who want rides but just a dozen Uber drivers, surge

pricing would allow the drivers to charge a higher price = low supply of drivers,

high demand from passengers. There are both advantages and disadvantages to

this. In the short term, some passengers might wish they were paying less and

some drivers might wish they were charging more. In the long run, however, this

surge pricing is technically more economically efficient than a fixed price because it takes into account the ever changing factors of supply and demand.

This type of dynamic pricing based on supply and demand is also used elsewhere. For example, dinner items on a restaurant menu are often more expensive than the same items for lunch. Restaurants that get more customers for dinner than lunch can charge a higher price at dinner for the same pasta dish = high demand for pasta, low limited supply of pasta. The price of a major commodity like oil is also based on supply and demand. In 1973, when the Organisation of Arab Petroleum Exporting Countries (OPEC) decreased the supply of oil they exported to countries like the United States, there was a huge oil crisis as prices went from $3 per barrel to $12 per barrel and the US went into a recession. US demand for oil was high, so OPEC limiting the supply of oil exported to the United States caused the price to skyrocket. Hotel rooms are also priced similarly. If you are going to a popular vacation destination over the summer season, the demand for those rooms is higher and the supply of hotel rooms fixed. So the same hotel rooms are going to be more expensive during holiday seasons vs. off-peak seasons. Watching a film in a cinema earlier in the day will likely be cheaper than watching the same film in the evening. Football tickets are more expensive for championship games rather than regular season games.

None of these situations are perfect, but they are more efficient markets than a *command economy*, where the government has complete control over resource allocation, deciding what goods and services to produce, their quantity, and their price. There are many examples of this dynamic pricing based on supply and demand, but not in the music industry. Record labels or streaming platforms operate their own kind of command economy by deciding what music to produce, their quantity, and their price. But just like Uber rides, oil prices, and hotel rooms, your love for music is heavily dependant on supply and demand. I would argue that as human beings, our 'demand' for music has stronger variations than for any other product in the world.

Fans Value Musicians Differently

How does this topic of pricing, supply, and demand work in music? Let's use Justin Bieber as an example instead of oranges. Some people in this world would pay £1000 to see Justin Bieber in concert. Others wouldn't go to his concert if the tickets were on sale for £1, or even if they were free. You can see this illustrates a huge difference between fans and non-fans.

In the example below, we have built out a matrix for two people—Person A and Person B. Each person attaches a different value to Justin Bieber tickets. Some of Justin Bieber's most intense fans call themselves 'Beliebers.' Person A is a Belieber and Person B is a Non-Belieber. So we can think of this table as the Belieber Matrix.

	Face Value Concert Ticket Price	Value to Specific Person
A - Justin Bieber Fan (Belieber)	£100	£1000
B - Justin Bieber Non-Fan (Non-Belieber)	£100	£1

- For Person A Belieber, paying £100 for a concert ticket that they would be willing to pay £1000 for means that they are getting a very good deal.

- For Person B Non-Belieber, paying £100 for a concert ticket is a terrible deal since they personally value a Justin Bieber ticket at £1.

This next table shows the added value for each person, measuring how much extra 'happiness' that person receives from the transaction. The fan gets lots of benefit from this situation, and the non-fan receives no benefit. Value is added for the fans but it doesn't necessarily hurt non-fans.

	Face Value Concert Ticket Price	Value to Specific Person	Added Value
A - Justin Bieber Fan (Belieber)	£100	£1000	£900
B - Justin Bieber Non-Fan (Non-Belieber)	£100	£1	0

Now picture yourself as a fan entering two different scenarios:

Scenario 1: You go online to a ticketing website and spend £100 on tickets to a Justin Bieber concert, which is a non-negotiable price set by the ticketing website.

Scenario 2: You go directly to Justin Bieber to buy a ticket to his concert and since he sees how big of a Belieber you are, how much 'demand' you have for that ticket, he gives you two tickets for the price of one. He may appreciate you as a fan so much that you get invited to an exclusive launch party for his next album. Now you have a ticket for both yourself and a fellow Belieber for just £100, and an even closer relationship with your favourite artist.

The problem is, scenario 2 doesn't really exist in the music industry.

You may have access to second-hand ticket auctions with varying prices but as a consumer, you do not have a direct relationship with your favourite artists. Likewise, most artists do not have direct access to you. A world with more direct relationships between all fans and artists would be beneficial for everyone.

If every musician had the ability to build a strong, direct relationship with their fans, could they provide different people with different products at different prices? And would this more accurately reflect the actual value people put on music? Wouldn't Justin Bieber want to reward his most passionate Beliebers with something extra, something different, something special?

To use terms from the field of economics, what I'm highlighting here are producer surplus, consumer surplus and price discrimination. Basically, people value things differently and therefore it makes sense for different things to be priced differently. This ideal state exists in economics textbooks and in the dreams of professors, but not the real world. Some situations do come close and we have an opportunity here for blockchain to bring a more efficient economic state by pricing art based more on supply and demand.

Different Values, Different Tokens

The extreme situation between Martin Shkreli and the Wu-Tang Clan highlights this challenge of economics in the music industry. Martin Shkreli's demand for Wu-Tang music was so high that he was willing to pay literally millions of dollars for their album. At the same time, other fans had similarly strong desires to hear the new Wu-Tang album but did not have millions of dollars to pay for the album. So how can we price or value art appropriate to each person's preferences? The answer comes from tokenisation, enabled by blockchain technology. This doesn't solve all problems, but it is a step in the right direction.

Particularly in the world of art and creativity, the relative value each of us puts on artwork can vary dramatically. You see these consumer preferences play out especially in the music industry since music is such a personal topic tied to our own identity. That's why some concerts can be excruciatingly boring and other concerts can be the some of the best nights of your life. Music is an expression of ourselves, our culture, our identity.

In 2014, the artist Taylor Swift wrote an op-ed piece in the Wall Street Journal outlining her vision for the music industry:

"It's my opinion that music should not be free, and my prediction is that individuals artists and their labels will someday decide what an album's price point is. I hope they don't underestimate themselves or undervalue their art. The way I see it, fans view music the way they view their relationships. Some music is just for fun, a passing fling (the ones they dance to at clubs and parties for a

month while the song is a huge radio hit, that they will soon forget they ever

danced to). Some songs and albums represent seasons of our lives, like

relationships that we hold dear in our memories but had their time and place in

the past. However, some artists will be like finding "the one." We will cherish

every album they put out until they retire and we will play their music for our

children and grandchildren. As an artist, this is the dream bond we hope to

establish with our fans."

Taylor is conveying this idea of relative value, and the blockchain provides

us with technology to accurately capture that value. It creates the opportunity to

price music and creativity at an individual, peer-to-peer level. This is one of the

many reasons why people refer to blockchain as the impending 'Internet of

Value.'

Blockchains of Creative Value

So if the Wu-Tang Clan released a Wu-Tang Token, they would be issuing a digital unit of value attached to the Wu-Tang Clan. One token could provide you access to special events, merchandise, retail partnerships, offers, or anything else the Wu-Tang Clan would want to provide in this direct-to-fan relationship. The market value of a token would be based on supply and demand, and may rise or fall depending on the overall success of the group's activities. So if the demand for work from the Wu-Tang Clan increases across the world, so should the price of their token. And if you own tokens, you could sell them to make a profit.

Let's say the Wu-Tang Clan releases 1 billion tokens into the market at a price of $0.01 per token. You could afford to invest in the Wu-Tang entity with the intention of funding their business & art and hopefully getting a return on your investment through increases in the overall token price. By spending $100 of your own money on Wu-Tang tokens, you would now own 10,000 tokens that are attached to the value of the Wu-Tang Clan. From the Wu-Tang Clan's perspective, they now have a new way to communicate directly with their fans. They could include in the token purchase process a set of questions about the token buyer to get more information about the fan's preferences. Now the group has more data about what fans are willing to pay for different artistic projects and could even deliver personalised offers to their fans. These tokens are essentially digital units of data. The potential user data attached to a token (with that data given voluntarily by fans) could be the strongest possible feedback loop for artists to understand what their fans really want. While many people have issues sharing their data with the government or social media platforms, I suspect that super fans would be much more willing to share intimate data with their favorite artists.

Even if Martin Shkreli was able to spend $2 million worth of his own money on buying Wu-Tang Tokens, this doesn't make Wu-Tang Tokens inaccessible to everyone else. The Wu-Tang Clan can manage their own economy by deciding how many tokens they want to create, what special benefits they would provide, and what information fans would need to share about their preferences. And the relative value of each artist to each person gives the people the freedom to buy whatever tokens and however many tokens they want. Some people may not buy any tokens at all and still enjoy the benefits of passively listening to an artist's music. Some people may buy an index of classic rock tokens or Italian disco tokens to support a music genre rather than individual. Some people may spread their money across Taylor Swift, Beyonce, and Rihanna tokens. And some people might pour all their money into buying Kanye West tokens. Each of these decisions are some combination of a person's love for the music and their desire for responsible financial investments. In fact, Martin Shkreli could still be satisfied by throwing his money around and getting something most other fans cannot get. This already happens today. Mariah Carey was paid £2.5 million to sing at the wedding of Irene Kogan, daughter of a Russian oligarch. If the wealthiest fans are willing to purchase millions of tokens, I am sure each artist could still work out some unique, personalised experience. The new token business model for artists continues to allow for wealthier fans to receive special benefits, but adds entirely new levels of engagement and empowerment for your average fan.

This is where things really get interesting. This means that all relationships in art could be priced at an individual peer-to-peer level. Maybe Wu-Tang Tokens could have a sliding scale of benefits. People who own 100 tokens might get a 10% lifetime discount on all Wu-Tang Merchandise. People who own 1000 tokens might get guaranteed tickets to all concert performances. People who own 10000 tokens might get exclusive access to a private Wu-Tang party. As an artist, you can pretty much make your own rules about how you want those tokens to function for your fanbase. And as a fan making an investment, the more you are willing to pay your artists will actually result in you receiving more benefits from your musical heroes. Martin Shkreli could still spend $2 million on Wu-Tang Tokens, but a 13 year-old Wu-Tang Clan fan can still listen to their music and still receive new benefits by spending even just $20 on Wu-Tang Tokens.

The already famous, already successful Wu-Tang Clan may easily sell millions of tokens around the world if they were to do an ICO. However, for a young country singer performing in small bars around Texas, selling even just a few hundred of her tokens may be that 'startup capital' she needs to fund her career. Many musicians are left behind not because their music doesn't have appeal, but because they are unable to secure the funding to market, promote, and manage their careers. There is often a huge disconnect between good art and financially successful art. Some groups of people hold the passionate opinion that the most famous, financially successful music is often the worst music!

Throughout the 20th Century, most artists have outsourced the business aspects of their career to record labels. This new 'token model,' innovates a step beyond the 'record label model,' and most importantly—it breaks assumptions we have about how artists can find success. You can extract more financial value from a small, committed group of fans through a token model rather than a record label model, which prioritises mass scale audience and clings to traditional business.

Civalringz, lead producer of *Once Upon A Time in Shaolin*, addressed this on the album's website,

"When recorded music loses its monetary value, it's the little guy who suffers most. Artists at the top of the tree have other potential revenue streams. They can tour, they can license, synchronize, and diversify into fashion or film.

68

But an independent musician starting out has none of those options. He needs the

thousand copies of his album to be worth something. Recorded music is the work

of art."

Scooter Braun is the founder of SB Projects, an entertainment and media

company that has managed artists including Justin Bieber, Ariana Grande, and

Martin Garrix. Scooter discovered Justin Bieber by stumbling upon one of his

YouTube videos in 2007 and was immediately able to identify his raw talent.

Through coaching, managing and helping Justin channel his artistic energy,

Scooter was able to turn Justin Bieber into one of the biggest pop stars of all

time. Jimmy Iovine, co-founder of Beats by Dre and Interscope Records, has

done the same thing throughout his career. As a producer for bands like

Fleetwood Mac, U2, and No Doubt, Jimmy's sound engineering and overall

coaching helped these groups reach new levels of success. Scooter Braun and

Jimmy Iovine played another important function - providing their artists with

initial working capital and managing their marketing. In South Korea, this end-

to-end artist management has become a highly efficient machine. A handful of

large companies such as SM, YG, and JYP have created comprehensive music factories that completely manage all aspects of a popstar's career from beginning to end, which has helped fuel the global boom of K-Pop over the past few years. Without someone like Scooter Braun, Jimmy Iovine, or a giant K-Pop company coaching you, how do you reach mainstream success? For every Justin Bieber serendipitously discovered on Youtube, there are hundreds of others who are left behind.

This situation exists for all types of artists. Without access to the most exclusive galleries and art shows, you will have a tough time making it as an artist. Without the financial buffer to explore your craft and develop as a photographer or author, your chances for success are low. We tend to accept and romanticise the idea of a 'starving artist' in our society. Arguably, a different skill set is needed to think in commercial terms vs. artistic terms. It's a widely held belief that making a business out of your art is incredibly hard. We overlook the detrimental effects of this reality because there is currently no better way to put a price on art in our economy. There is no alternative. However, in a world where you can finance artists directly through tokens, supporting them as their patron/ shareholder/fan, you are improving the likelihood that even the most obscure artists can provide value to some individuals across the global market economy. The wealthy Medici Family funded those artists in the 15th Century because no one else could. In an open internet economy, we all have the ability to fund art. A carefully created system of new incentive structures allows every individual in our society to experiment with tokens to fund things we care about.

Some specific types of artists are in an almost perpetual state of financial ruin. For example, ballet companies usually survive only by relying on grants or taking a chance that regular donations will keep coming. Ballet performances may never sell out with mainstream audiences, but there are a committed enough group of fans who could pay for more than just tickets and in return receive more benefits. Ballet company tokens could find enough buyers within this committed fan group to support their creative activities with much more consistency than their current business model. In some ways, you could say that society already subsidises the arts through the public organisations dedicated to promoting the arts that are funded by taxes. By enhancing this model through tokenisation, the taxpayers already indirectly funding creativity could now receive more benefits through art-related tokens and increased incentives to see more art succeed. A world where each citizen in society more directly funds creativity and more directly benefits from its output is a world I want to live in.

This is a new kind of direct relationship we can build between artists and fans, a new environment that can place a new layer of value for the artists in our society. We could more accurately value art. As a self-proclaimed fan of hip hop, Shkreli could continue paying large sums of money to support his favourite hip hop artists through token purchases. If he owns Wu-Tang Tokens, he benefits financially from the increasing value of the hip hop group across all of their activities and not just by holding the one album *Once Upon A Time In Shaolin*.

Blockchain technology can be a truer measure of value for artwork and enable better compensation for artists. Ideally, if we have artwork of all types better valued, then society as a whole should be able to place a higher, more accurate value to artists. Right now, art is undervalued in terms of its contribution to society. While not every artist can be as big as The Wu-Tang Clan, there is a huge long tail of artists of all types who could benefit from a new way to monetise their creativity. I believe that blockchain, when applied to the music industry, can restore and reinvigorate creativity by giving everyone in society an

opportunity to be not only a patron, but a shareholder of the arts.

5. Technology in Action

"I will take fate by the throat, it will never bend me completely to its

will."

-Ludwig von Beethoven

The Rise of Independent Artists

Something happened at the 2017 Grammy Awards that shocked the entire

music industry. A new independent artist emerged to win three Grammy Awards

without the backing of any major record label. His name was Chancelor Jonathan

Bennett, better known as Chance the Rapper. At the time Chance was 23 years

old, had been nominated for seven Grammys, and ended up winning Best Rap

Performance, Best Rap Album, and Best New Artist.

Chance won Best Rap Album for his independently released mixtape

Coloring Book, which was also the first time a streaming-only album has ever qualified for a Grammy nomination. All three of Chance's mixtapes have been released as completely free digital downloads without any record label backing.

When Chance went onstage to accept the award for Best New Artist, it signalled both his arrival to mainstream music fame and the arrival of a new business model for artists to imitate. Chance showed us that another avenue exists for monetising your art, an avenue where he himself took on responsibilities without the need for traditional gatekeepers and middle men. Chance had actually turned down numerous offers from record labels, and ended up proving to the world that it was possible for musicians to take more control of their own business.

In a 2017 interview with Vanity Fair, Chance outlined his approach to building a music career:

"After I made my second mixtape and gave it away online, my plan was to sign with a label and figure out my music from there. But after meeting with the three major labels, I realized my strength was being able to offer my best work to

people without any limit on it...I make money from touring and selling

merchandise, and I honestly believe if you put effort into something and you

execute properly, you don't necessarily have to go through traditional means."

Chance isn't the only one doing this. In 2016, acclaimed artist Frank Ocean

was in the process of buying himself out of his contract with Def Jam Records.

As a condition of letting him go, Def Jam claimed the distribution rights to his

next album *Endless*. And so Frank released *Endless* as an avant-garde visual

album, exclusive to Apple Music. What he did next could be interpreted as a slap

in the face to his former record label, something both controversial and

masterful.

Literally one day after releasing *Endless* through Def Jam, Frank Ocean

released a completely separate album called *Blonde*, which he released

independently. Def Jam Records therefore lost out on all the revenue from

Blonde, which ended up being one of the most critically and commercially

successful albums of the year. And because Frank Ocean was not tied to a record

label in releasing *Blonde*, he personally received a significantly higher percentage of revenue.

To accompany the release of *Blonde*, Frank opened pop-ups shops in New York, London, Chicago and Los Angeles that contained both the album and a glossy magazine named *Boys Don't Cry*. The magazine was a 360-page publication featuring essays, interviews and various artwork in collaboration with a dozen different artists. Frank Ocean had taken complete responsibility for the marketing and promotion of his album, a service generally handled by the record labels. Frank Ocean no longer felt the need to work with a record label in order to sell music, and he had proven himself correct.

Years before Frank Ocean and Chance the Rapper's bold moves towards independence, the band Radiohead took a groundbreaking approach with their 2007 album *In Rainbows*. Radiohead's six-album contract with record label EMI had just ended and the band decided to release their next album independently. They came up with the bold experiment to make their album available as a digital download and tell fans that they could buy the album for whatever price they wanted, even £0. Radiohead hosted the album exclusively on their website www.inrainbows.com, not selling it anywhere else. There was also a second version of the album with extra features in what was called 'discbox' format, available through their website at a price of £40.

The band took control of production, distribution, marketing and even the pricing of their album. In the music value chain, the record label middlemen were taken out of the equation. The incentive for online music pirates was also removed, because Radiohead was basically giving away their music for free. Despite this counterintuitive business model, *In Rainbows* was actually a huge financial success for the band, winning two Grammy Awards and becoming the #1 album on the charts in many different countries.

In some ways, you could consider this the literal opposite approach compared to the RZA, who created only one copy of the Wu-Tang Clan album and auctioned it off to the highest bidder. RZA had created a tightly controlled environment to distribute his music. Radiohead made their music freely available for everyone at any price.

Whether intentional or not, Radiohead had managed to set up a real-life economic experiment exploring game theory. It's crazy—these are the kinds of experiments economists write about in books but rarely get a chance to see in real life. Each person interested in the album could pay literally whatever they wanted. We discussed earlier how the relative value of something is different per person, but in Radiohead's case they could see the literal relative *financial* value of their music when each person paid a different price.

Some diehard Radiohead fans may have paid hundreds or thousands of pounds, others may have downloaded the album for free, and many people probably sat somewhere in the middle. Radiohead received stronger signals of who was buying their album, which provided them with more data & insight to segment their fans into different groups.

Hypothetical Radiohead Fan Segments

Fan Type	Album Price	What The Fan Paid
A - Casual Fan	Whatever you want	£0-1
B - Strong Fan	Whatever you want	£1-39
C - Super Fan	Whatever you want	£40+

Radiohead's lead singer Thom Yorke commented on the success of *In Rainbows* in a 2007 interview with Wired magazine,

> *"In terms of digital income, we've made more money out of this record than out of all the other Radiohead albums put together, forever—in terms of anything on the Net. And that's nuts. It's partly due to the fact that EMI wasn't giving us any money for digital sales. All the contracts signed in a certain era have none of that stuff."*

That last sentence from Thom Yorke describes how the band's older record contracts with EMI did not factor in digital sales. This is incredibly shocking—

Radiohead was missing out on available revenue opportunities purely because their record contracts were too old fashioned, which is quite crazy. It shows that you cannot rely on record labels to keep up to date with the technology that impacts your business as an artist. This is an overarching theme throughout the music industry. The examples above from Chance the Rapper, Frank Ocean, and Radiohead are iterations in original thinking and an artist's willingness to try something new, away from record labels. What experiments will come next?

There are always shifting tides in the way that artists deliver music to their fans and commercialise their work. I predict that the biggest trend we will continue to see is the decentralisation of power within the music industry, as artists decouple from record labels and find other ways to monetise their art. As this happens inevitably, blockchain will be the technological tool that artists use to build direct relationships and monetise independently.

"Industry rule number four thousand and eighty, record company people are shady."

"Check The Rhime" by A Tribe Called Quest

I believe blockchain technology is the most underleveraged tool for all the different stakeholders in the music business, especially the artists. A consistent underlying theme is the concept of *value*. We each value different things at different prices and in our society, music & art is where we find the most extreme differences in opinion about relative value.

If RZA were to revisit his intentions behind releasing *Once Upon a Time in Shaolin*, perhaps now he could approach future Wu-Tang music through a blockchain release instead of creating a single album owner through Martin Shkreli. For the other gatekeepers in the music industry like the record labels, let's explore new ways to approach releasing music that can satisfy the broader music industry ecosystem.

The world moves at the pace of technology and only a handful of individuals and companies are keeping up with that pace by examining the bold frontiers between music and technology. These people are already building a future that more accurately places value on art and puts more power in the hands

82

of artists and their fans. Let us examine ways that artists are building upon the benefits blockchain can help bring to the music industry: traceability, compensation, and tokenisation.

The Blockchain Music Startup Landscape

A handful of blockchain startups are looking at the dual problems of traceability & compensation. Some of leaders behind this are people with deep roots within music, including the artist Imogen Heap, who has a long history of being forward thinking in the music industry. She has released most of her music independently and even released her own hardware products, such as the mi.mu gloves that create music out of movement. She was also the first musician to use smart contracts to get paid for her music. Today, she is the founder of a new blockchain startup called Mycelia.

In an interview with Forbes, she described her vision of Mycelia:

> *"I dream of a kind of Fair Trade for music environment with a simple one-*

stop-shop portal to upload my freshly recorded music, verified and stamped, into the world, with the confidence I'm getting the best deal out there, without having to get lawyers involved."

The name Mycelia comes from a type of fungus that stretches deep underground and all across the world, emblematic of how she hopes that the idea of a shared musical database for artists can be a global solution.

The Mycelia team is about to launch Mycelia's flagship project called Creative Passport, activating this through a 40-city world tour including interactive exhibitions, talks, and live concerts. Creative Passport is essentially a digital ID that contains all the specific data and metadata attached to an artist. This is hosted on a blockchain as an immutable, traceable record, a connective tissue for all stakeholders in the music industry. With a decentralised blockchain database, everyone in the music industry can have a creative passport that we can all verify. This will help secure artist copyright and create a consistent record that currently does not exist. Mycelia plans to make the Creative Passport free to all music makers and charge a fee for businesses to access the Creative Passport blockchain database for insights and marketing purposes. Those businesses might be streaming services like Spotify or record labels or anyone interested in artist data. The ambition for Mycelia is to create more transparency and traceability for artists.

_____Soundpruf is an application that will allow passionate music fans to better understand their unique listening habits, earn tokens for supporting emerging artists, and provide those artists, the ones who need it most, with an entirely novel revenue channel. The team is also developing a platform that gives fans a chance to invest in artists they believe in through blockchain-enabled security tokens.

"We think blockchain opens a number of hugely exciting doors when it comes to redefining and rewarding what's valuable in the music world. With a little imagination, smart contracts can enable both fans and artists to transform the meaning and impact of a stream, a full album, a video, a ticket, a concert— ultimately, a career."

—Alex Nordenson, Co-Founder and CEO of Soundpruf

Other projects include Choon, a blockchain company started by British DJ Gareth Emery. The Choon platform will be a streaming service that returns a higher revenue percentage for artists and enables the creation of smart contracts to make royalty payments. Under the topic of royalties, accounting, and compensation, the company Music Coin has created a free platform for people to listen to music while encouraging fans to tip artists in cryptocurrency. TokenFM employs a similar model where you can pay musicians in cryptocurrency that subsequently helps fund their projects and other artistic experiences. Blockchain startup Ujo, funded by Consensys Ventures, *"uses blockchain technology to create a transparent and decentralized database of rights and rights owners, automating royalty payments using smart contracts and cryptocurrency."* They are working quite closely with record labels, helping co-found the new Capital Innovation Center at Capital Records.

Resonate is another startup that allows users to buy tokens in order to stream music on a model they call #stream2own, *"a method of slowly increasing price as a fan comes to love a song, starting really cheap until finally reaching the price of a normal download."* It's an interesting new take on the economics of streaming. People have to pay in credits for every time they stream a song, but first stream is always the cheapest, priced at .002 credits on their platform. The price to stream doubles to .004 credits for the second play, then doubles again to .008 credits for the third play. The price keeps doubling each time you play a song again until costing 1.022 for the ninth play. By the time you play a song for the ninth time, the song is completely 'paid for,' payment is no longer required for any future plays and now the song is free. The incentive here is for fans to engage in greater discovery of new songs and new artists since the first stream is the cheapest stream. If a fan enjoys an artist's music, they will be supporting their music more with each successive play. In theory, your relative love for a particular song is more accurately priced that current streaming platforms that charge you the same amount for each song. Resonate says this is a much better situation for artists, particularly new artists, and overall costs fans a similar amount of money when compared to mainstream music streaming platforms.

The company Vezt is taking the ICO model and creating Initial Song Offerings (ISOs), a method to allow fans to acquire rights in their favourite songs through purchasing tokens. Each token you purchase gives you a fractional percentage of an artist's royalties tied to that song. Buy buying a token, you are helping fund artists and creating a new way to interact between artists and fans. By operating as a digital marketplace, Vezt is creating a new form of financing for artists and a new way for fans to financially benefit from investing in artists. The world of blockchain music startups is crowded, and I don't know which of the above companies will succeed. But I'm happy that there is so much excitement around the ability for blockchain technology to solve the intrinsic problems within the music industry.

As we look forward to the potential within each of these startups to improve the music industry, it's worth looking back to the infamous rise of Napster in 1999, the world's pioneer in peer-to-peer file sharing services. Napster allowed people to download and share music for free, which many record labels and artists considered to be 'theft.' Napster was famously sued into oblivion by the music industry establishment, including notable lawsuits from the Recording Industry Association of America (RIAA) and the band Metallica. After reaching 80 million users within a couple of years, the resulting litigation was too much and Napster filed for bankruptcy in 2002.

I remember using Napster years ago. The thrill of downloading music for the very first time was an unforgettable experience. While I still admire the pirate-like gusto coming from Napster founders Sean Fanning and Sean Parker, I can understand the negative reaction from the music industry. Napster was directly challenging the music establishment and revenue opportunities were unclear for the artists. With the current generation of blockchain startups, we see entrepreneurs actually seeking partnerships with artists, streaming platforms, or record labels. Having artists understand the benefits of the technology is critical to the success of these blockchain startups.

Direct-to-Fan Relationships & Tokenisation

While Traceability & Compensation are clearly problems that need to be addressed, the next topic of tokenisation is about exploring a new way to think about music. How can artists develop new ways to make money, no matter their level of fame? How can artists and fans develop stronger, more direct relationships with each other?

Technology has enabled us to connect more easily with people all around the world. Whether you are using Facebook to speak with a family member overseas, arguing with a stranger on Reddit, or leaving gushing YouTube comments for your favourite bands, our ability to live online has made our world smaller. Technology has broken down communication barriers and brought us closer to the people we care about. Why can't technology bring us even closer to the artists and fans we care about?

Ryan Leslie has always been a multi-faceted music pioneer. As a young boy, Ryan entered Harvard University at the age of 15 and was so focused on pursuing music that his studies suffered and he was put on academic probation several times. After graduation, Ryan worked for many years as a producer with Sean "Diddy" Combs under his label Bad Boy Records and then on his own as a musical artist. His first few albums were released under Universal Motown until he eventually parted ways with the record label in 2010. Afterwards, Ryan started releasing music independently and has since made unique efforts to build direct relationships with his fanbase.

His 2013 album *Black Mozart* was released directly on his own website through his fan club called Renegades Club. Fans who paid $12.00 for membership to Renegades Club were able to download the album, had their details added to Ryan Leslie's personal address book, and were encouraged to reach out to Ryan and his team directly. He was creating a new type of digital fan relationship. In addition to building stronger relationships with his fans, Ryan creates unique business opportunities for himself. On his website, Ryan sells merchandise and tickets to special events like his private New Year's Eve party, described as "*An unforgettable 18-hour experience with round trip travel from Frankfurt, Germany to the legendary palace in Vienna, Austria on Ryan's privately chartered Airbus A319 commercial jet.*" Tickets are limited and prices range from around $175 for the cheapest package to around $3500 for the most expensive VIP package.

Ryan Leslie is a great case study of someone who has taken a truly unique approach to engaging directly with his fans. His most recent venture is called

SuperPhone, a sophisticated mobile app for artists to keep in touch with their fans through text messaging. If you look up Ryan Leslie on Twitter, you will find this message on his bio, *"Literally always available via email or text: r@mzrt.com or +16467982928."*

If you text that number, you will be adding yourself to Ryan's version of SuperPhone. SuperPhone allows him to manage the tens of thousands of fans who have actually reached out to him through text message. He built the product as a way to make his customer relationship management (CRM) process much more effective. Whenever someone sends that first text, they are asked to share their information with Ryan. In return, the app provides fans with constant updates about events and album releases while also targeting fans with personalised offers. Through this app, Ryan can filter and build different customer segments. He can create a more sophisticated marketing relationship with his fans through actual data & insight. He is refining some of the most advanced forms of digital marketing and making it personal for his own fans. Ryan's goal is to make SuperPhone the app of choice for any major artist managing their fanbase, which Ryan pursues through his own company

Disruptive Multimedia.

Legendary Silicon Valley venture capitalist and hip hop aficionado Ben Horowitz is an investor. Horowitz has said *"Ryan is a genius and is about to transform the music industry and rebalance it in favor of the artists."*

This mobile optimised, digital fan club idea has paid off for Ryan. He has managed to make $2 million in revenue from relationships with roughly 15,000 fans. You need to take a deep breath in order to realise what this means, not only for Ryan but as a possibility for all artists. To draw an analogy with businesses in the tech industry, many mobile apps can increase their revenue in two ways:

1) Increase the number of users on your platform, charging each person the same amount.

OR

2) Increase the amount you charge each person on your platform, no matter how many people are on the platform. This is also known as increasing average revenue per user (ARPU).

If Ryan made $2 million from 15000 fans, his average revenue per user (ARPU) or perhaps 'average revenue per fan' (ARPF) is about $133. Each Ryan Leslie fan has given roughly $133 in exchange for his merchandise, experiences, or artwork. Ryan doesn't rely on the indifferent non-fans, but instead doubles down on his superfans. Ryan is an example of someone who has seen how different fans are willing to pay different amounts and has created a business out of that. Ryan may not have the level of fame as Taylor Swift, but he proves that you don't necessarily need millions of fans to 'make it' in the music industry. You just need enough fans that care about you enough to pay you enough.

To make a million dollars, you could get a million people to pay you one dollar each or get one thousand people to pay you one thousand dollars each. Ryan Leslie has pursued a strategy related to getting a smaller group of fans to pay more instead of a larger group of fans to pay less. For those wanting to explore this concept further, I highly recommend the essay 1000 True Fans, written by the founding editor of Wired Magazine Kevin Kelly. If we take a step back and take a look at the broader music industry, that second option of increasing ARPF is rarely ever considered. Ryan Leslie is an example of someone who has thought about the world differently.

If Ryan Leslie could offer one more thing on top of Superphone, I would suggest tokenisation. He could launch another method to reach his fans directly by creating Ryan Leslie tokens and attaching special experiences to owning them. As a refresher, releasing Ryan Leslie crypto tokens could have several benefits:

- Ryan can raise funds (in typical fiat currency or cryptocurrency) through an initial coin offering (ICO), giving him a quicker injection of capital to fund his different artistic projects.
- People all across the world have the ability to invest in Ryan's ICO and build a new type of relationship with their beloved artist, something that previously did not exist.
- Both Ryan and his fans/token-holders would benefit financially from any subsequent success from Ryan's work, as the token value would also increase in price.

Going back to revenue growth strategies, there are two business approaches Ryan might consider if he were to release his own token:

1) Increasing the number of people who buy Ryan Leslie tokens.

OR

2) Increasing the value of a single Ryan Leslie token, which translates into greater token value for all token holders, no matter how many or how few there are.

Ryan's focus on option 2 is what he is already doing with Superphone, which translates smoothly into a crypto token strategy. Ryan is already crafting greater and more direct experiences for his fans. He is not as focused on getting a million new fans but instead providing even more value for his current group of fans. This combined approach of artist tokenisation and increasing revenue per fan rather than number of fans could improve how we conceptualise the music business. One of the biggest benefits for a fan could be a direct relationship with Ryan Leslie that is even more personalised. Not only could Ryan offer a sliding scale of benefits based on how many tokens you have purchased, but he could also make your benefits completely customised towards your own preferences. This is a brand new business model for artists.

While Ryan Leslie has been doing his own version of building direct-to-fan relationships without blockchain technology, the electronic music artist Gramatik is an example of someone who has embraced blockchain and the idea of tokenisation. Gramatik put together his own ICO in November 2017, launching the cryptocurrency GRMTK and raising $2 million in 24 hours. By owning GRMTK tokens, you actually own rights and royalties to Gramatik's music proportional to the number of tokens you own. Gramatik has been creating a modern version of his own tribe, enabling his fans to rally around him in the form of a crypto token. Tokenisation is kind of like crowdfunding, but one step further. It's literally the opposite of record labels owning artists, because artists like Gramatik share and distribute 'ownership' across their fans. Since the March 2018 announcement of Wu-Tang member Ol' Dirty Bastard's son launching a crypto currency, the most recent development from October 2018 is that Young Dirty has made progress. He is in the process of launching AltMarket, a peer-to-peer cryptocurrency trading and fundraising platform creating Initial Artist

Offerings (IAOs). Starting with Ol Dirty Bastard Coin (ODB), purchasing these tokens will allow fans to fund artwork, buy special merchandise, and access special events. The team behind AltMarket hope that this will begin a new wave of tokenisation for all types of artists. Whether through AltMarket or other similar blockchain startups, artist tokenisation is coming to a platform near you.

Sebastian Junger is an author and US Military veteran who wrote the 2016 book *Tribe: On Homecoming and Belonging*. Through the lens of anthropology, Junger outlines that within each of us, we all feel a powerful human tendency of wanting to belong to a tribe, some kind of small group with a shared purpose. He uses examples ranging from Native American tribes to soldiers as examples of modern 'tribes' where people have an almost intrinsic programming to feel deep connection and attachment. Junger examines how our psychology creates patterns of behaviour that influences every decision we make. If we have these very human needs for belonging and identity, it seems to be a natural progression that we look towards our favourite heroes or artists to satisfy those needs.

If each artist adopts a system of tokenisation and creates their own token, they now have a method to build an even stronger version of their own 'tribe.' I think we would all gravitate towards our favourite artists—our heroes—the same way we search for identity through countries, universities, sports teams, or religions. This tokenisation can work for any group trying to attract other people, starting with music fans. The trend of tokenisation is something all groups can utilise to build even stronger bonds between their members. As the saying goes, your vibe attracts your tribe.

We began explaining the concept of relative value and demand by using the example of 'Beliebers,' a nickname for superfans of Justin Bieber. People from the 'tribe' of Justin Bieber self-identify as Beliebers. This tribe creation is widespread across the music industry, with each fan group giving themselves a brand name attached to their identity. Selena Gomez fans are called 'Selenators.' Jimmy Buffett fans are called 'Parrotheads.' Lady Gaga fans are called 'Little Monsters.' Insane Clown Posse fans are called 'Juggalos.' Beyonce has her 'Beyhive.' Imagine if each of these modern tribes was able to rally around a token tied to their favourite artist. This is not limited to the music industry. Famous Bollywood actor Salman Khan has a group of fans who call themselves

'Salmaniacs.' Fans of the animated television show My Little Pony are called 'Bronies.' Jennifer Aniston fans are called 'Fanistons.' Fans of the football club Arsenal are called 'Gooners.' Tokenisation can truly impact not just the music industry but all forms of art, creativity, and entertainment. The demand for tokenisation exists because it is directly tied to our psychological desire to belong to a tribe.

6. A Portrait of The Future Artist

"I'd rather be a pirate, than join the navy."

-Steve Jobs

Whose World Is This? The World Is Yours

Legal conflicts in the music industry happen all the time and often read like plot lines to a soap opera. In an infamous public display in the mid 1990s, the artist Prince wrote the word 'SLAVE' in big bold letters across his face to convey the message that record contracts are like slavery. The singer Toni Braxton declared bankruptcy in 1998 despite selling $188 million worth of CDs. She had a terrible record deal where she was paid less than 35 cents per album sold. Other famous artists who have sued their record labels include: Lil Wayne, Wiz Khalifa, John Fogerty, Kesha, Dr. Dre, Backstreet Boys, 'NSYNC, Dixie Chicks, Childish Gambino.

I highlight these numerous examples to illustrate a broken system that is stacked against the artists. We need a new system that prioritises the artists first. Think about the creativity that is able to flourish when artists aren't so firmly locked into old paradigms of the music business—like Chance the Rapper, Frank Ocean, or Ryan Leslie.

The singer Courtney Love wrote an impassioned essay in Salon magazine in 2000 outlining her problems with the music industry. It's a wonderfully written, extensive article that is probably just as valid in its criticism today as it was eighteen years ago. I would encourage everyone interested in the business of music to read the piece.

At one point she hightights the role of record labels in the face of changing technology,

"Being the gatekeeper was the most profitable place to be, but now we're in a world half without gates. The Internet allows artists to communicate directly

with their audiences; we don't have to depend solely on an inefficient system

where the record company promotes our records to radio, press or retail and then

sits back and hopes fans find out about our music.

If a record company has a reason to exist, it has to bring an artist's music

to more fans and it has to deliver more and better music to the audience. You

bring me a bigger audience or a better relationship with my audience or get the

fuck out of my way. Next time I release a record, I'll be able to go directly to my

fans and let them hear it before anyone else."

Not only does Courtney Love chastise the record labels, but she also

outlines new responsibilities for artists to take control of their own careers due to

the possibilities afforded by internet technology. Fittingly, Spotify just announced

on September 20, 2018, that they would allow artists to directly upload their

music to the streaming platform, without the need to go through record labels.

The tools to take control of your business as an artist will continue to grow. In a

world where traditional methods of 'outsourcing' your marketing to record labels

clearly leaves you at risk, we need new types of artists who embrace both art and

business. If the history of strained relationships between artists and record labels is a consistent theme, what does the future hold? If we view the decentralisation of power in the music industry as a good thing, we should view blockchain technology as a good thing.

If I were to start my own music career today from scratch, my strategy would be to build a direct-to-fan relationship, underpinned by a foundation of blockchain technology that allows me to trace my digital copyright and be compensated fairly. I would immediately 'tokenise' myself as an artist and raise funds through an initial coin offering (ICO). My tokens would be available for anyone in the world to purchase, whether you are a casual fan, superfan, or someone in between. The money raised in the ICO would go towards funding my artistic projects, combining the ideas of patronage, crowdfunding, and being a shareholder. For my fans, these tokens would give you access to special merchandise, unique offers, and exclusive access, all proportional to the number of tokens you own. Smart contracts would dynamically pay out royalties based on an immutable shared ledger of my music's data and metadata. The fans who have invested in my tokens would benefit from token utility and the potentially increasing value of the tokens based on what I am able to accomplish. Fans would develop a stronger relationship with me as a musician and would now have additional financial incentives tied to my own success, making them a cutting-edge version of a brand ambassador for my art. My biggest fans would purchase lots of tokens and reap the benefits, and yet the more passive fans could still benefit from hearing my music without needing to buy tokens. A stronger reward for stronger fans is what I would want and I would work towards making my strongest fans happy rather than aiming to please everyone. This is a portrait of the future artist.

What if you, as a fan, could invest in this kind of direct relationship with your favourite artist—Chance the Rapper, Radiohead, Prince, or someone else? Or maybe you could invest in building a direct relationship with a young, unknown artist who very few people believe in except for you? If we can build new direct-to-fan/direct-to-artist relationships with blockchain technology, we can build the bold future of music and art. Music will be a leading indicator of all art forms as the decentralisation of power within creative industries continues. These solutions are within our grasp and it's just a matter of time before they are brought to market. As we have examined, there are already artists like Ryan

Leslie, Imogen Heap, or Chance the Rapper, who are carving new paths in a world that does not yet exist.

Venn Diagrams & Pandora's Box

"I know that people think independence means you do it by yourself, but

independence means freedom."

Chance the Rapper, during his Best New Artist Grammy acceptance speech

To build upon the words of Chance the Rapper, independence for a musician means freedom from the people who make it difficult for you to monetise your art. The music industry is littered with these people, bloated chains of middlemen that create severe trust issues in terms of access, data, and compensation. It's no secret that there are challenges within the music industry for both artists and fans and in order to move things forward, we need more venn diagrams.

What is a venn diagram? It's a diagram that highlights the overlap between two different areas that are combined to create a brand new area. I consider the human version of a venn diagram to be a kind of person who doesn't just embrace one identity or one field of expertise, but instead carves out a unique perspective combining two fields or skillsets. We are often told that specialising in one field is the right thing to do for your career. Society is very quick to put people into categories and boxes - you are 'just' a rapper, 'just' an accountant, 'just' a graphic designer, but terms don't commonly exist for someone who may fit into several categories. We are often told to classify ourselves as either left-brained or right-brained and rarely a mixture of the two. My belief is that in the world today, the most successful artists will not only be artists, but also savvy businesspeople. People who are both artists and technologists will create the tools that utilise blockchain to improve traceability, compensation, and tokenisation for the music industry. Chance the Rapper, Frank Ocean, and Ryan Leslie are venn diagrams. They have taken responsibility not just for the creation of their music but also the business aspects of their art. The future of the music world belongs to people who are venn diagrams. To ensure progress for everyone, we need more venn diagrams. We need more venn diagrams of musicians and technologists, of left-brains and right-brains, teams and combinations of people who can address society's problems from their own respective, different backgrounds.

The wealthiest musicians are ones who have expanded beyond selling music and into other business ventures. Hip hop artist Dr. Dre has made more money from his company Beats by Dre, which was acquired by Apple in 2014 for $3 billion, than any previous work producing and releasing music. It's a similar situation for rapper Jay-Z, whose business exploits include a sports management agency, the music streaming service Tidal and the clothing label Rocawear. Sean "P. Diddy" Combs started his career as a producer/rapper and now has an estimated net worth of $900 million due to a combination of successes ranging from his record label Bad Boy Records, his clothing line Sean John, and his stake in vodka brand Cîroc.

Beyond hip hop, Sir Elton John owns Rocket Entertainment, a group composed of an artist management company, a sports management agency, and a film & theatre production company. U2 lead singer Bono is a managing partner at private equity firm Elevation Partners, focusing on new media and technology investments. Singer Jimmy Buffett has an estimated net worth of $550 million, largely due to a business empire consisting of his Margaritaville restaurants, hotels, and casinos. In the world today, the most successful artists cannot just think about their music, but will also need to consider their business. The lead singer of the band Iron Maiden, Bruce Dickinson, is another venn diagram. He owns Cardiff Aviation, an airplane maintenance, repair, and pilot training company. He formed the beer brand Trooper Craft Ale, a joint venture between Iron Maiden and Robinsons Brewery that is sold in 50 countries. He has registered Iron Maiden LLP as a company, which was named one of the fastest growing companies in the UK in 2013.

Prometheus Unbound

As we look to the future, I'm going to make the prediction that hip hop artists will be at the cutting edge of the blockchain movement. This new type of artist for the 21st Century will emerge from the hip hop genre first, because leading figures from the world of hip hop have always been at the technological forefront. The rapper Nasir 'Nas' Jones launched his own venture capital fund

QueensBridge Venture Partners in 2014 and has subsequently invested in some of the most successful tech companies of the last decade, including Dropbox, Lyft, and Coinbase. He has developed a friendship with Ben Horowitz, one of the most prominent venture capitalists in Silicon Valley who also has a longstanding connection with the hip hop industry. Both Nas and Horowitz are venn diagrams of hip hop and technology. And most importantly, they have been proponents of Bitcoin and blockchain technology for years. Nas told the blockchain media publication Coindesk in 2014, *"Bitcoin will evolve into an industry as big, if not bigger, than the Internet. My man Ben Horowitz really opened my eyes to that point."* Through Queensbridge Venture Partners, Nas helped fund the blockchain startup BlockCypher, among other blockchain/crypto investments. Hip hop was born out of the struggle of some of the poorest neighbourhoods in the United States. A common thread within the lyrics is financial independence representing an artist emerging out of their troubled background. If you can characterise hip hop as a musical genre all about the hustle, entrepreneurship, and one-upmanship, it might explain a natural affinity between hip hop and cryptocurrency. The rapper Snoop Dogg publicly declared his willingness to accept Bitcoin as early as 2013 and has performed at numerous blockchain conference afterparties. Countless rappers, perhaps more than any other type of

musical artist, have endorsed or included cryptocurrency within their lyrics such

as Royce 5'9", Big Baby Gandhi, and Nipsey Hussle.

Blockchain and cryptocurrencies represents not only an opportunity for the

hip hop industry, but underrepresented minority groups. A January 2018 survey

conducted by the Global Blockchain Business Council showed that over half of

the owners of Bitcoin in the United States are people of colour. The rapper Mims

has been associated with the promotion of the startup RecordGram, which won

the top startup award at TechCrunch Disrupt's December 2017 Start Up

Battlefield competition. RecordGram was the first music based app to win the

contest and also the first time a founder of colour had won the competition.

Through the app, people can create and upload beats to then lease to aspiring

artists. The inspiration for Mims comes from his own personal experience in the

music industry. In a type of story we have heard before, Mims felt disillusioned

with the music industry after his 2007 hit *"This Is Why I'm Hot"* brought roughly

$18 million in revenue that year for Capitol Records, but Mims ended up earning

only $30,000. Mims has been an early proponent of blockchain technology and has integrated the music cryptocurrency Tune Token within RecordGram, citing many of the blockchain benefits we have discussed at length in this book. This token tracks royalties automatically (traceability) and facilitate payments (compensation). Mims and the team behind RecordGram/Tune Token represent the forefront of technology startups. The track record of rappers, first with Bitcoin adoption and now broadening into Blockchain, gives me hope that whatever the music industry looks like in five years, it will be driven by hip hop artists.

I began this book with the example of the Wu-Tang Clan and Martin Shkreli because the crazy situation represents the broader challenges within the music industry. It also represents where I think we will find the solution. I predict that the mainstream adoption of blockchain technology for the entire music industry will come through the leadership of hip hop artists. The collective energy of hip hop channeled into developing benefits for all creative industries is a majestic power. But sincerely, whether the earliest adopters of blockchain are the rappers, the K-Pop stars, or the Bollywood actors, I truly believe that the world of art and creativity needs blockchain technology.

The *Once Upon a Time in Shaolin* album was kept in a stunningly ornate, highly secure silver box, a fitting statement for such a grand work of art. Though if we widen our eyes and take a step back we can see that there is another box that has been opened for the world—the Pandora's Box of blockchain technology. The entire range of new possibilities available for artists, fans, and entrepreneurs has arrived. Blockchain technology has been unleashed upon the world and I look forward to seeing what comes next.

On the website created especially for *Once Upon A Time in Shaolin,* RZA & Civalringz wrote a long note explaining the concept behind the album:

"Perhaps it is our cultural attitudes to modern music that have cast it as something to be consumed. The complacency of no holds barred access and the saturation wrought by technology's erosion of challenges. Mass replication has fundamentally changed the way we view a piece of recorded music, while digital universality and vanishing physicality have broken our emotional bond with a piece of music as an artwork and a deeply personal treasure.

By adopting an approach to music that traces its lineage back through the Enlightenment, the Baroque and the Renaissance, we hope to reawaken age old perceptions of music as truly monumental art. In doing so, we hope to inspire and intensify urgent debates about the future of music, both economically and in how our generation experiences it. We hope to steer those debates toward more radical solutions and provoke questions about the value and perception of music as a work of art in today's world."

Blockchain can provide the '*radical solution*' for music in order to restore artists to the '*profoundly high esteem*' they received in previous eras and to once again make music a '*truly monumental art.*'

With such a powerful statement, I get the feeling this is not the last we will be hearing from the Wu-Tang Clan about how they plan to shape the future of the music industry. And for anyone doubting this, let us not forget the important message we learned from one of their most famous songs, the Wu-Tang Clan Ain't Nothing to Fuck With.

Acknowledgements

Writing a book for the first time, I needed as much help as possible. I am blessed to have such talented, helpful, and intelligent people in my life who were able to look over drafts, assist with research, and provide relevant feedback. I'm a huge fan of technology and the arts, and if you have made it this far I hope that you enjoyed the book and have been inspired to perhaps think just a little bit more about these topics and how you can shape their impact on society.

Special shout out goes to Roxanne Somboonsiri, Hamdan Azhar, Devika Wood, Leslie Ching, Vanessa Bakewell, Deven Patel, Koen Bosma, Lewis Harland, Alvin Carpio, Nikhil Vadgama, Daniel Dippold, Greg West, Florent Hacq, Ken Uehara, Guilherme Silva, Stuart Brown, Christine Ng, James Butcher, Simone Colayco, Graham Hindle, Colleen Sullivan, Christopher Grant, Ashley Zandy, Natalie Brieger, Lewis Gyson, Ali Samir, Shahryar Khan, Malcolm Clark, Martin Clark, Myra Nizami, Conner Sherline, Jake Schonberger, Nikita Paschenko, Areeq Chowdhury, Pierre Du Toit, Etienne Brunet, Rob Cooke, Anik Mathur, Aakarsh Ramchandani, Noble Lano, Anil Clifford, Kristina Tauchmannova, Sheelah Odedra, Christopher Davis, Emma Ryan, Illya Kondratyuk, Daniele Mensi, Samir Goel, Mahoney Turnbull, Alvin James, Halsey Huth, Christian Del Rosario, Kristian Else, William Kim, Nick Jenkins,

Jillian Kowalchuk, Hasani Ade, Rich Serunjogi, Hilary Maguire.

A Frontier X publication.

Selected Bibliography

1. The Wu-Tang Clan & Martin Shkreli

Jordan Bassett, "Wu-Tang's $2m Album Comes With A Bizzare Clause: The Rap Group - Or Bill Murray - Are Entitled To Steal It Back In A Heist" *NME* 10 December 2015. <https:// www.nme.com/blogs/nme-blogs/wu-tangs-2m-album-comes-with-a-bizarre-clause-the-rap- group-or-bill-murray-are-entitled-to-steal-it-13108>

Allah Sha Be, "Man seeks $1 million from Wu Tang Clan over stolen artwork for 'Once Upon A Time In Shaolin' Album" *The Source* 12 April 2018. <http://thesource.com/ 2018/04/12/man- seeks-1-million-from-wu-tang-clan-over-stolen-artwork-for-once-upon-a-time-in-shaolin- album/>

Cyrus Bozorgmehr, *Once Upon a Time in Shaolin: The Untold Story of the Wu-Tang Clan's Million-Dollar Secret Ablum, the Devaluation of Music, and America's New Public Enemy No. 1* (Flatiron Books, 2017).

Colin Campbell, "Hillary Clinton fumes at controversial CEO who jacked up drug price: 'So Mr. Shkreli, what's it going to be?'" *Business Insider* 28 September 2015. <http:// uk.businessinsider.com/hillary-clinton-martin-shkreli-daraprim-price-2015-9>

Stephanie Clifford, "Martin Shkreli Is Jailed for Seeking a Hair From Hillary Clinton" *The New York Times* 13 September 2017. <https://www.nytimes.com/2017/09/13/ business/dealbook/ martin-shkreli-jail.html>

Trace William Cowen, "Lil Wayne Reportedly Threatening to Sue Martin Shkreli If He Leaks More 'Carter V' Tracks" *Complex* 18 May 2017. <https://www.complex.com/music/ 2017/05/ lil-wayne-threatening-sue-martin-shkreli-if-leaks-carter-v-tracks>

Rian Daly, "Wu-Tang Clan reportedly sued for $1 million over one-of-a-king album 'Once Upon A Time In Shaolin'" *NME* 11 April 2018. <https://www.nme.com/news/ music/wu-tang-clan- sued-1-million-one-kind-album-upon-time-shaolin-2289587>

Lilly Dancyger, "Despicable 'Pharma Bro' Martin Shkreli's Terrible Deeds: A Timeline" *Rolling Stone* 9 January 2017. <https://www.rollingstone.com/culture/culture-news/ despicable- pharma-bro-martin-shkrelis-terrible-deeds-a-timeline-126114/>

Steve Dent, "Wu-Tang Clan sell its one-of-a-kind 'Shaolin' album for millions" *Engadget* 25 November 2015. <https://www.engadget.com/2015/11/25/wu-tang-clan-shaolin-album- millions/>

Chris Graham, "Martin Shkreli - 'American's most hated man' - auctioning off chance to hit him in the face" *The Telegraph* 28 September 2016. <https://www.telegraph.co.uk/ news/ 2016/09/27/martin-shkreli---americans-most-hated-man---auctioning-off-chanc/ >

Sarah Rense, "Martin Shkreli's Shakespearean Downfall: A Timeline" *Esquire* 17 December 2015. <https://www.esquire.com/news-politics/news/a40577/martin-shkreli-

arrest-timeline/>

Colin Stutz, "Martin Shkreli Offers Kanye West $10M for 'The Life of Pablo'" *Billboard* 2 November 2016. <https://www.billboard.com/articles/columns/hip-hop/6874864/martin- shkreli-offers-kanye-west-10-million-the-life-of-pablo>

Luke Timmerman, "A Timeline of the Turing Pharma Controversy" *Forbes* 23 September 2015. <https://www.forbes.com/sites/luketimmerman/2015/09/23/a-timeline-of-the-turing- pharma-controversy/#227ab008771d>

Alex Young, "Bill Murray is not legally allowed to steal back Wu-Tang's album, but he should anyways" *Consequence of Sound* 10 December 2015. <https://consequenceofsound.net/   2015/12/bill-murray-is-not-legally-allowed-to-steal-back-wu-tangs-album-but-he-should-   anyways/>

http://scluzay.com

http://scluzay.com/eighteight

2. Introducing Blockchain

W. Joseph Campbell, "'The Internet? Bah!' Classic off-target essay appeared 20 years ago" *Poynter* 27 February 2015. <https://www.poynter.org/news/internet-bah-classic-target-essay- appeared-20-years-ago>

Faisal Hoque, "3 Ways VC Funding Could Destroy Your Company" *Business Insider* 16 May 2014. <https://www.businessinsider.com/vc-funding-could-destroy-your-company-2014-5? IR=T>

Bernard Marr, "How Blockchain Will Transform The Supply Chain And Logistics Industry" *Forbes* 23 March 2018. <https://www.forbes.com/sites/bernardmarr/2018/03/23/how- blockchain-will-transform-the-supply-chain-and-logistics-industry/#6dc12e295fec>

Metamorph, "100 Reasons Why Venture Capital is Dead" *Metamorph* 11 July 2018. <https:// medium.com/   @metamorph_io/100-reasons-why-venture-capital-is-dead-44017a80ea32>

Satoshi Nakamoto, "Bitcoin: A Peer-to-Peer Electronic Cash System" <https://bitcoin.org/bitcoin.pdf>

Jason Rowley, "Where venture capitalists invest and why" *TechCrunch* 9 November 2017. <https://techcrunch.com/2017/11/09/local-loyalty-where-venture-capitalists-invest-and- why/>

George S, "Asset Tokenization on Blockchain Explained in Plain English" *Coinmonks* 19 May 2018. <https://   medium.com/coinmonks/asset-tokenization-on-blockchain-explained-in-plain-   english- f4e4b5e26a6d>

Houman Shadab, "What are Smart Contracts, and What Can We do with Them?" *Coin Center* 15 December 2014. <https://coincenter.org/entry/what-are-smart-contracts-and-what-can-we-do- with-them>

Clifford Stoll, "Why The Web Won't Be Nirvana" *Newsweek* 26 February 1995. <https://

www.newsweek.com/clifford-stoll-why-web-wont-be-nirvana-185306>

Valentina Zarya, "Female Founders Got 2% of Venture Capital Dollars in 2017" *Fortune* 31 January 2018. <http://fortune.com/2018/01/31/female-founders-venture-capital-2017/>

Changpeng Zhao, "ICOs - Not Just "Good-to-Have," But Necessary." 27 May 2018. https:// www.linkedin.com/pulse/icos-just-good-to-have-necessary-changpeng-zhao/

"A Beginner's Guide to Smart Contracts" *Block Geeks* <https://blockgeeks.com/guides/smart- contracts/>

3. Music On A Blockchain

Kaleem Aftab, "Sixto Rodriguez: The builder who's bigger than Elvis" *The Independent* 24 July 2012. <https://www.independent.co.uk/arts-entertainment/music/features/sixto-rodriguez- the-builder-whos-bigger-than-elvis-7966151.html>

Sha Be Allah, "Altmarket Launches Cryptocurrency Exchange, Opens Pre-Sale For O.D.B. Coin" *The Source* 24 October 2018. <http://thesource.com/2018/10/24/altmarket-launches- cryptocurrency-exchange-opens-pre-sale-for-o-d-b-coin/>

Ed Christman, "Black Box Royalties Myths, Common Misconceptions Debunked at Music Biz 2018" *Billboard* 15 May 2018. <https://www.billboard.com/articles/business/8456271/black- box-royalties-myths-panel-music-biz-2018>

Annabella Coldrick, "Spotify Profit Payouts: What's The Fairest Way To Recompense Artists?" *Music Business Worldwide* 4 September 2018. <https://www.musicbusinessworldwide.com/ spotify-profit-payouts-whats-the-fairest-way-to-recompense-artists/>

Ken Consor, "What You Didn't Know About Radio Royalties" *Songtrust* 6 August 2014. <https://blog.songtrust.com/publishing-tips-2/what-you-didnt-know-about-radio-royalties>

Eustace Cryptus, "Wu-Tang Clan Are Releasing A Cryptocurrency In Honor Of Ol' Dirty Bastard" *Bitcoinist* 24 October 2018. <https://bitcoinist.com/wu-tang-clan-are-releasing-a- cryptocurrency-in-honor-of-ol-dirty-bastard/>

Cory Doctorow, "The point of Patreon isn't how many people earn a full-time living, it's how much of the money from art goes to artists" *BoingBoing* 8 December 2017. <https:// boingboing.net/2017/12/08/measuring-the-right-thing.html>

Max Foreman, "Music Royalties Explained" *Pro Audio Files* 11 April 2018. <https:// theproaudiofiles.com/music-royalties-explained/>

Andy Greene, "Rodriguez: 10 Things You Don't Know About the 'Searching for Sugar Man' Star" *Rolling Stone* 28 March 2013. <https://www.rollingstone.com/music/music-news/ rodriguez-10-things-you-dont-know-about-the-searching-for-sugar-man-star-99288/>

Peter Harris, "The quest for accurate streaming royalties data" *Res()nate* 25 August

2016. <https://resonate.is/seeking-streaming-royalties-data/>

Stan Higgins, "Wu-Tang Clan Rapper's Son to Launch Cryptocurrency" *CoinDesk* 26 March 2018. <https://www.coindesk.com/son-of-wu-tang-clan-rapper-is-launching-a-cryptocurrency>

Tim Ingham, "The Odds Of An Artists Becoming A 'Top Tier' Earner On Spotify Today? Less Than 1%" *Music Business Worldwide* 25 March 2018. <https://www.musicbusinessworldwide.com/the-odds-of-an-artist-becoming-a-top-tier-earner-on-spotify-today-less-than-1/>

C. Edward Kelso, "Music Streaming Service Arena Pays Royalties in Bitcoin to Eliminate Industry Black Box" *Bitcoin.com* 8 October 2017. <https://news.bitcoin.com/music-streaming-service-arena-pays-royalties-in-bitcoin-to-eliminate-industry-black-box/>

Sean Michaels, "Rodriguez lawsuit aims to uncover cause of singer's missing royalties" *The Guardian* 6 May 2014. <https://www.theguardian.com/music/2014/may/06/rodriguez-lawsuit-missing-royalties-searching-for-sugar-man>

Lee Ann Obringer, "How Music Royalties Work" *HowStuffWorks* <https://entertainment.howstuffworks.com/music-royalties6.htm>

Nilay Patel, "How the Music Modernization Act will help artists get paid more from streaming" *The Verge* 2 October 2018. <https://www.theverge.com/2018/10/2/17927852/music-modernization-act-streaming-monetization-meredith-rose-vergecast>

Emily Price, "More than 1 million people are supporting creators on Patreon, up from 500k last year" *Fast Company* 17 May 2017. <https://www.fastcompany.com/4038149/more-than-1-million-people-are-supporting-creators-on-patreon-up-from-500k-last-year>

Peter Resnikoff, "Paradise Distribution Estimates That 97% of 'Black Box' Royalties Can Be Resolved & Paid" *Digital Music News* 9 October 2018. <https://www.digitalmusicnews.com/2018/10/09/paradise-distribution-black-box/>

Ben Sisario, "Now That 'Sugar Man' Is Found, Lawsuit Focuses on Missing Royalties" *The New York Times* 2 May 2014. <https://www.nytimes.com/2014/05/03/business/media/now-that-sugar-man-is-found-lawsuit-focuses-on-missing-royalties.html>

Soundreef, "How does a collecting society split royalties?" *Soundreef* 26 September 2013. <http://www.soundreef.com/en/blog/how-does-a-collecting-society-split-royalties/>

Soundreef, "Music royalties in the UK: a quick guide" *Soundreef* 25 April 2014. <http://www.soundreef.com/en/blog/music-royalties-in-the-uk-a-quick-guide/>

Roy Trakin, "Rodriguez Label Chied: 'Our Dealings with Clarence Avant Were Always Positive'" *Billboard* 13 June 2014. <https://www.billboard.com/articles/news/6121152/rodriguez-label-chief-our-dealings-with-clarence-avant-were-always-positive>

Todd Van Der Werff, "Trump signs the Music Modernization Act, the biggest change to copyright law in decades" *Vox* 11 October 2018. <https://www.vox.com/culture/

2018/10/11/17965690/music-modernization-act-copyright-law-licensing-streaming>

Amy Wang, "The Music Modernization Act Is One Step Closer to Fixing Music Copyright" *Rolling Stone* 28 June 2018. <https://www.rollingstone.com/music/music-news/the-music-modernization-act-is-one-step-closer-to-fixing-music-copyright-666938/>

Noah Yoo, "Ghostface Killah Launches His Own Cryptocurrency" *Pitchfork* 6 October 2017. <https://pitchfork.com/news/ghostface-killah-launches-his-own-cryptocurrency/>

https://www.prsformusic.com/help/how-do-you-use-music-recognition-technology-to-track-dj-performances
https://www.prsformusic.com/help/how-do-you-collect-and-calculate-royalties
https://www.copyrightuser.org/create/creative-process/going-for-a-song-track-6/
https://www.royaltyexchange.com/learn/music-royalties
https://www.soundexchange.com/advocacy/music-modernization-act/
https://wutangcoin.com/

4. The Economics of Value

Kimberly Amadeo, "OPEC Oil Embargo, Its Causes, and the Effects of the Crisis" *The Balance* 6 November 2018. <https://www.thebalance.com/opec-oil-embargo-causes-and-effects-of-the-crisis-3305806>

Lightsey Darst, "The Poorest Art: Dance And Money (II)" *Huffington Post* 4 August 2012. <https://www.huffingtonpost.com/lightsey-darst/ballet-culture-money-salary_b_1562729.html>

Jennifer Dunning, "Dance and Profit: Who Gets It?" *The New York Times* 20 September 2003. <https://www.nytimes.com/2003/09/20/arts/dance-and-profit-who-gets-it.html>

Stefan Kyriazis, "Guess how much stars get paid to sing at weddings? Mariah makes TWICE as much as Elton" *Express* 16 January 2017. <https://www.express.co.uk/entertainment/music/754985/Wedding-singer-Mariah-Carey-Elton-John-paid-how-much-Russian-oligarch-most-expensive>

Nicole Loeffler-Gladstone, "Do Ballet Companies Make (Financial) Sense?" *Pointe Magazine* 29 November 2001. <https://www.pointemagazine.com/do-ballet-companies-make-financial-sense-2412809969.html>

PYMNTS, "What's Old Is New Again: Surge Pricing" *PYMNTS* 9 January 2018. <https://www.pymnts.com/commerce/2018/uber-surge-pricing-ridesharing-retail-gebni/>

Rory Satran, "inside the rihanna navy: her most extreme super-fans speak out" *i-D* 31 July 2016. <https://i-d.vice.com/en_us/article/xwxn73/inside-the-rihanna-navy-her-most-extreme-super-fans-speak-out>

Taylor Swift, "For Taylor Swift, the Future of Music Is a Love Story" *Wall Street Journal* 7 July 2014. <https://www.wsj.com/articles/for-taylor-swift-the-future-of-music-is-a-love-story-1404763219>

https://www.eia.gov/finance/markets/crudeoil/supply-opec.php

5. Technology in Action

Josh Constine, "SuperPhone is building a Salesforce for texting" *TechCrunch* 29 January 2018. <https://techcrunch.com/2018/01/29/crm-for-sms/>

Kevin Kelly, "1000 True Fans"4 March 2008. <https://kk.org/thetechnium/1000-true-fans/>

Julian Mitchell, "Ryan Leslie's SuperPhone: Beating Facebook To The Scalable Personal Messaging Table" *Forbes* 25 January 2016. <https://www.forbes.com/sites/julianmitchell/2016/01/25/ryan-leslies-superphone-beating-facebook-to-the-enterprise-messaging-table/#178c848fccbb>

Lisa Robinson, "Why Chance the Rapper Makes Music for Free (and How He Actually Makes Money)" *Vanity Fair* February 2017. <https://www.vanityfair.com/hollywood/2017/02/why- chance-the-rapper-music-is-free-and-how-he-makes-money>

Eliot Van Buskirk, "Thom Yorke Discusses 'In Rainbows' Strategy With David Byrne" *Wired* 19 December 2017. <https://www.wired.com/2007/12/thom-yorke-disc/>
http://soundpruf.com
https://resonate.is/
https://resonate.is/stream2own/
https://musicoin.org/
https://token.fm/
https://genius.com/B-horowitz-playlist-for-fortune-magazine-annotated
https://mzrt.com/
https://mzrt.com/products/renegades-club-membership

6. A Portrait of The Future Artist

Sadaf Ahsan, "How on God's green earth is P. Diddy the highest earning celebrity in 2017 (2017!!!)?" *National Post* 13 June 2017. <https://nationalpost.com/entertainment/celebrity/ how-on-gods-green-earth-is-p-diddy-the-highest-earning-celebrity-in-2017-2017>

Allana Akhtar, "Here's How Much Jay-Z Is Worth—and How He Makes Money" *Time* 22 January 2018. <http://time.com/money/5108647/jay-z-net-worth/>

Daniel Applewhite, "Founders And Venture Capital: Racism Is Costing Us Billions" *Forbes* 15 February 2018. <https://www.forbes.com/sites/forbesnonprofitcouncil/2018/02/15/ founders-and-venture-capital-racism-is-costing-us-billions/#300c54742e4a>

Jono Bacon, "Iron Maiden's Bruce Dickinson on Entrepreneurialism, Adventure, and Managing Adversity" *Forbes* 27 November 2017. <https://www.forbes.com/sites/jonobacon/ 2017/11/27/iron-maidens-bruce-dickinson-on-entrepreneurialism-adventure-and-managing- adversity/#4f4990a64b71>

Bloomberg, "This Is What The Average Bitcoin Owner Looks Like" *Fortune* 24 January

2018. <http://fortune.com/2018/01/24/young-men-buying-bitcoin/>

Eric Boehlert, "Pearl Jam: Taking on Ticketmaster" *Rolling Stone* 29 December 1995. <https:// www.rollingstone.com/music/music-news/pearl-jam-taking-on-ticketmaster-67440/>

C. Vernon Coleman II, "A Brief History Of Hip-Hop's Connection To Cryptocurrency" *XXL* 12 March 2018. <http://www.xxlmag.com/news/2018/03/history-hip-hop-connection- cryptocurrency/>

Lauren deLisa Coleman, "Inside The Powerful Intersection Of Hip Hop And Cryptocurrency" *Forbes* 30 March 2018. <https://www.forbes.com/sites/laurencoleman/ 2018/03/30/inside-the- powerful-intersection-of-hip-hop-and-cryptopcurrency/ #38bce55f4679>

Javier E. David, "Nas is like…half man, half venture capitalist" *CNBC* 6 February 2016. <https://www.cnbc.com/2016/02/06/nas-is-likehalf-man-half-venture-capitalist.html>

Nikhilesh De, "Rapper Mims to Promote 'Tune' Token for Artists" *CoinDesk* 10 May 2018. <https://www.coindesk.com/this-is-why-cryptos-hot-rapper-mims-to-promote-blockchain- for-artists>

Joseph Diaz, "Confessions of a Diva: Toni Braxton Reveals Story Behind Bankruptcy Headlines" *ABC News* 30 November 2012. <https://abcnews.go.com/Entertainment/toni-braxton-reveals- story-bankruptcy-headlines/story?id=17839154>

Zack O'Malley Greenburg, "This App Is Why Mims Is Hot (Again)" *Forbes* 20 October 2017. <https://www.forbes.com/sites/zackomalleygreenburg/2017/10/20/this-app-is-why-mims- is-hot-again/#194c793446a9>

Aric Jenkins, "Rapper 50 Cent Says He Isn't Actually a Bitcoin Millionaire" *Fortune* 27 February 2018. <http://fortune.com/2018/02/26/50-cent-bitcoin-millionaire/>

Courtney Love, "Courtney Love does the math" *Salon* 14 June 2000. <https:// www.salon.com/ 2000/06/14/love_7/>

Sheldon Pearce, "What's Behind Rap's Love Affair With Cryptocurrency" *Pitchfork* 22 May 2018. <https://pitchfork.com/thepitch/whats-behind-raps-love-affair-with-cryptocurrency/>

Alexis Petridis, "Elton John: 'Our kids aren't stuck in a mansion. We go to Pizza Hut.'" *The Guardian* 7 February 2016. <https://www.theguardian.com/music/2016/feb/07/ elton-john-i-really-hate-the-cult-of-celebrity>

Emily Price, "Jimmy Buffett Is More Business Than Booze These Days" *Fortune* 8 February 2018. <http://fortune.com/2018/02/08/jimmy-buffett-margaritaville-business/ >

Nathan Richter, "What Your Business Can Learn from Iron Maiden" *Monetate* 8 January 2014. <https://www.monetate.com/blog/what-your-business-can-learn-from-iron-maiden>

Pete Rizzo, "Hip-Hop Icon Nas: We're Entering the Age of Bitcoin" *CoinDesk* 1 August 2014. <https://www.coindesk.com/hip-hop-icon-nas-coinbase-age-of-bitcoin>

Ben Schiller, "Why Venture Capitalists Aren't Funding The Businesses We Need" *Fast Company* 28 September 2017. <https://www.fastcompany.com/40467045/why-venture-capitalists-arent-funding-the-businesses-we-need>

Alexandra Topping, "Iron Maiden: too hairy for pop but still turning metal into gold" *The Guardian* 29 November 2013. <https://www.theguardian.com/music/2013/nov/29/iron- maiden-metal-gold-uk-economic-recovery?CMP=fb_gu>

Nastia Voynovskaya, "Paid In Full: How the Rap World Embraced Bitcoin" *KQED* April 3 2018. <https://www.kqed.org/arts/13827706/paid-in-full-how-the-rap-world-embraced-bitcoin>

Dennis Wafula, "Hip Hop Artist Mims Launched RecordGram App, A Blockchain Platform For Artists" *Cryptona* 12 May 2018. <https://cryptona.co/hip-hop-artist-mims-launches- recordgram-app-a-blockchain-platform-for-artists/>

Phil Wahba, "How Iron Maiden's Bruce Dickinson Rocks in Business" *Fortune* 23 December 2017. <http://fortune.com/2017/12/23/iron-maiden-bruce-dickinson-aviation-business/>

Global Blockchain Business Council, Annual Report 2018. <https://gbbcouncil.org/annual- report-2018>

https://www.gerryhemingway.com/piracy2.html

https://artists.spotify.com/blog/now-in-beta-upload-your-music-in-spotify-for-artists

CPSIA information can be obtained
at www.ICGtesting.com
Printed in the USA
BVHW030215271121
622650BV00006B/295

9 781793 086754